Raspberry Pi 2 Server Essentials

Transform your Raspberry Pi into a multi-purpose web server that supports your entire multimedia world with this practical and accessible tutorial!

Piotr J Kula

BIRMINGHAM - MUMBAI

Raspberry Pi 2 Server Essentials

First published: April 2016

Production reference: 1220416

Published by Packt Publishing Ltd.
Livery Place
35 Livery Street
Birmingham B3 2PB, UK.

ISBN 978-1-78398-569-2

www.packtpub.com

Credits

Author
Piotr J Kula

Reviewers
Ian McAlpine
Cédric Verstraeten

Commissioning Editor
Priya Singh

Acquisition Editors
Usha Iyer
Reshma Raman

Content Development Editor
Sanjeet Rao

Technical Editor
Jayesh Sonawane

Copy Editor
Yesha Gangani

Project Coordinator
Judie Jose

Proofreader
Safis Editing

Indexer
Monica Ajmera Mehta

Graphics
Disha Haria

Production Coordinator
Nilesh Mohite

Cover Work
Nilesh Mohite

About the Author

Piotr J Kula started his passion for computer technologies when he took apart his father's IBM PC/XT machine at the age of 6. It became clear that Piotr had a natural ability with technology after he reconstructed the machine, and it booted.

After 25 years, Piotr has worked for various companies in different countries. He has always solved complex problems or engaged in new experiences. As long as it had a processor of some sort, Piotr was always the first to try, fix, or configure it.

Today, Piotr is the CEO of his own company, Kula Solution Ltd., in the United Kingdom. Piotr is certified in several Microsoft technologies, and he specializes in Microsoft and Linux technologies.

Piotr's dream is for a unified experience between Linux and Microsoft. He has never been deterred by negativity from either side, and instead, he has strived to find a way to build a bridge between these distant giants. After discovering Raspberry Pi, he completely replaced every other embedded device that he owned and was successful at releasing *Raspberry Pi Server Essentials*, with *Packt Publishing*.

Today, Piotr is one step closer to fulfilling his dream with the release of *Raspberry Pi 2 Server Essentials*. This book is mostly about Linux, but it also talks about integrating and running Windows on your beloved Raspberry Pi.

I would like to thank Katarzyna Kula, my amazing wife who helps me decide when enough work, is enough! For always supporting me through all my projects and countless hours spent on my computers. I would also like to thank the entire Raspberry Pi community, especially the members on Stack Exchange, everybody at *Packt Publishing*, and those who helped me in various ways to complete this book.

About the Reviewers

Ian McAlpine's first introduction to computers was his school's Research Machines RML-380Z and his Physics teacher's Compukit UK101. This was followed by a Sinclair ZX81 and then a BBC Micro Model A, which he still has. This interest resulted in a MEng in Electronic Systems Engineering from Aston University and an MSc in Information Technology from the University of Liverpool. Ian is currently a product expert in the BI & Analytics Competency Centre, at SAP Labs, in Vancouver, Canada.

The introduction of Raspberry Pi not only rekindled his desire to *tinker* but also provided an opportunity to give back to the community. Consequently, Ian was a very active volunteer working on The MagPi, a monthly magazine for Raspberry Pi, which you can read online or download for free from `https://www.raspberrypi.org/magpi`. He also holds an amateur radio license (callsign VE7FTO) and is a communications volunteer for his local community Emergency Management Office. He was a technical reviewer for the *Raspberry Pi Cookbook for Python Programmers* and *Raspberry Pi Projects for Kids* books, both published by *Packt Publishing*.

I would like to thank my darling wife, Louise, and my awesome kids Emily and Molly for allowing me to disappear into my "office"... and for training our dog to fetch me!

Cédric Verstraeten is an MSc in Engineering who's primarily active in the C++ community. He works as a software engineer and is a huge open source enthusiast. He spends most of his time on side projects that can automate and simplify people's lives. He's the organizer of the Raspberry Pi Belgium meetup and the founder of the Open Source video surveillance system called Kerberos.io.

I would like to thank Packt Publishing for allowing me to be part of this as a reviewer. I really think their books can give people an in-depth overview of a particular topic.

www.PacktPub.com

eBooks, discount offers, and more

Did you know that Packt offers eBook versions of every book published, with PDF and ePub files available? You can upgrade to the eBook version at www.PacktPub.com and as a print book customer, you are entitled to a discount on the eBook copy. Get in touch with us at customercare@packtpub.com for more details.

At www.PacktPub.com, you can also read a collection of free technical articles, sign up for a range of free newsletters and receive exclusive discounts and offers on Packt books and eBooks.

https://www2.packtpub.com/books/subscription/packtlib

Do you need instant solutions to your IT questions? PacktLib is Packt's online digital book library. Here, you can search, access, and read Packt's entire library of books.

Why subscribe?

- Fully searchable across every book published by Packt
- Copy and paste, print, and bookmark content
- On demand and accessible via a web browser

Table of Contents

Preface

The purpose of this book is to get you started with Raspberry Pi, but this book has chapters focused on Raspberry Pi 2. The main goal here is to get your projects started with some solid hardware and programming tips, which are essential.

What this book covers

Chapter 1, Getting Started with the Raspberry Pi, will cover the basic equipment that we need to use with this book. We will have to look into other peripherals that we have bought to see how the Raspberry works. We will then see how to flash the newest Raspbian image to our SD card.

Chapter 2, Preparing a Network, will illustrate how to set up LAN and a wireless connection to our network to connect to the Internet. We will set some network benchmarks and understand some of its limitations. We will also look into Dynamic DNS hosting.

Chapter 3, Configuring Extra Features, will illustrate how to update the software and firmware of Raspberry Pi. You will learn about the watchdog and understand how to buy extra decoder licenses.

Chapter 4, Using Fast Web Servers and Databases, will illustrate how to set up a quick web server using nginx with PHP, and we can decide whether we want to use MySQL or SQLite.

Chapter 5, Setting Up the Raspberry Pi as a File Server, will illustrate how to attach and format a USB storage medium. We will not only look into the various ways of sending data to Raspberry Pi, but we will also understand how to share media on the network. As an extra task, we will look into creating the hardware RAID!

Chapter 6, Setting Up Game Servers, will explore open source game engines that are available on the repository. We will also have a sneak peek at the Jessie repository, which is in beta testing.

Chapter 7, Streaming Live HD Video, will explore the camera module and illustrate a simple technique to stream a video. This chapter contains exclusive streaming tutorials.

Chapter 8, Setting Up the Pi as a Media Center Server, will illustrate how to connect an HD monitor and play some videos that were recorded or stored earlier. We will also look into OSMC, and we will explore the benefits of running it as a dedicated media player.

Chapter 9, Running Your Pi from a Battery's Power Source, will explain the benefits of various types of battery technology and how to get the best performance without spending too much money.

Chapter 10, Windows IoT Core, is finally available on the embedded ARM, and it will explore the capabilities of running IoT as an Operating System with a basic programming tutorial with C#.

Chapter 11, Running Your ownCloud, will discuss how to install the ownCloud software on your Pi, and it will free you from privately owned services.

Chapter 12, The Internet of Things – Sensors in the Cloud, is more of a case study about how to complete your projects by storing accurate data accessible anywhere in the cloud.

What you need for this book

You need at least a Raspberry Pi 2 with a recommended 8 GB SD card, 1 amp micro USB power supply, and a network cable connected to a router with the Internet.

Who this book is for

Seeking inspiration for some new tech projects? Want to get more from your Raspberry Pi? This book has been created especially for you!

Conventions

In this book, you will find a number of text styles that distinguish between different kinds of information. Here are some examples of these styles and an explanation of their meaning.

Code words in text, database table names, folder names, filenames, file extensions, pathnames, dummy URLs, user input, and Twitter handles are shown as follows: "We can include other contexts through the use of the `include` directive."

A block of code is set as follows:

```
auto lo

iface lo inet loopback
iface eth0 inet dhcp
```

When we wish to draw your attention to a particular part of a code block, the relevant lines or items are set in bold:

```
allow-hotplug wlan0
auto wlan0

iface wlan0 inet dhcp
```

Any command-line input or output is written as follows:

```
sudo touch wpa_supplication.conf

nano wpa_supplication.conf
```

New terms and **important words** are shown in bold. Words that you see on the screen, for example, in menus or dialog boxes, appear in the text like this: "Clicking the **Next** button moves you to the next screen."

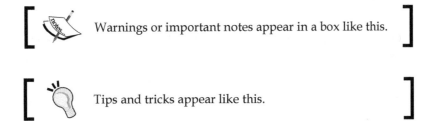

> Warnings or important notes appear in a box like this.

> Tips and tricks appear like this.

Reader feedback

Feedback from our readers is always welcome. Let us know what you think about this book—what you liked or disliked. Reader feedback is important for us as it helps us develop titles that you will really get the most out of.

To send us general feedback, simply e-mail feedback@packtpub.com, and mention the book's title in the subject of your message.

If there is a topic that you have expertise in and you are interested in either writing or contributing to a book, see our author guide at www.packtpub.com/authors.

Customer support

Now that you are the proud owner of a Packt book, we have a number of things to help you to get the most from your purchase.

Downloading the example code

You can download the example code files for this book from your account at http://www.packtpub.com. If you purchased this book elsewhere, you can visit http://www.packtpub.com/support and register to have the files e-mailed directly to you.

You can download the code files by following these steps:

1. Log in or register to our website using your e-mail address and password.
2. Hover the mouse pointer on the **SUPPORT** tab at the top.
3. Click on **Code Downloads & Errata**.
4. Enter the name of the book in the **Search** box.
5. Select the book for which you're looking to download the code files.
6. Choose from the drop-down menu where you purchased this book from.
7. Click on **Code Download**.

You can also download the code files by clicking on the **Code Files** button on the book's webpage at the Packt Publishing website. This page can be accessed by entering the book's name in the **Search** box. Please note that you need to be logged in to your Packt account.

Once the file is downloaded, please make sure that you unzip or extract the folder using the latest version of:

*   WinRAR / 7-Zip for Windows
*   Zipeg / iZip / UnRarX for Mac
*   7-Zip / PeaZip for Linux

Downloading the color images of this book

We also provide you with a PDF file that has color images of the screenshots/diagrams used in this book. The color images will help you better understand the changes in the output. You can download this file from `http://www.packtpub.com/sites/default/files/downloads/ RaspberryPi2ServerEssentials_ColorImages.pdf`.

Errata

Although we have taken every care to ensure the accuracy of our content, mistakes do happen. If you find a mistake in one of our books—maybe a mistake in the text or the code—we would be grateful if you could report this to us. By doing so, you can save other readers from frustration and help us improve subsequent versions of this book. If you find any errata, please report them by visiting `http://www.packtpub.com/submit-errata`, selecting your book, clicking on the **Errata Submission Form** link, and entering the details of your errata. Once your errata are verified, your submission will be accepted and the errata will be uploaded to our website or added to any list of existing errata under the Errata section of that title.

To view the previously submitted errata, go to `https://www.packtpub.com/books/content/support` and enter the name of the book in the search field. The required information will appear under the **Errata** section.

Piracy

Piracy of copyrighted material on the Internet is an ongoing problem across all media. At Packt, we take the protection of our copyright and licenses very seriously. If you come across any illegal copies of our works in any form on the Internet, please provide us with the location address or website name immediately so that we can pursue a remedy.

Please contact us at `copyright@packtpub.com` with a link to the suspected pirated material.

We appreciate your help in protecting our authors and our ability to bring you valuable content.

Questions

If you have a problem with any aspect of this book, you can contact us at `questions@packtpub.com`, and we will do our best to address the problem.

1
Getting Started with the Raspberry Pi

Connecting to a network should be as easy as plugging in a cable. The question is, what can we do on the Raspberry Pi after we are connected to the Internet or a local network? This is why it is essential to learn about the hardware prerequisites and capabilities of the Raspberry Pi, so that your idea is theoretically possible to accomplish. Also, knowing your hardware inside out will make troubleshooting problems much easier to deal with later in the book.

The most common problems associated with the Raspberry Pi are related to power. These problems can cause it to restart, cause unexpected behavior, or may show a rainbow screen during the boot process if you have an external monitor connected.

This chapter is all about identifying your Raspberry Pi and the peripherals that you are using or may want to use along with it. There are two main pieces of information you should know about your Raspberry Pi: the model and version.

Hardware requirements

This book assumes that you are using a Raspberry Pi 2, Model B.

The Raspberry Pi 2 is mostly backwards compatible with all its predecessors. Whenever a compatibility issue occurs, it will be made clear to the user and an alternative solution will be provided, if possible.

The latest versions of Raspberry Pi at the most basic level only need a power supply and Micro SD card to run. To make initial configurations easier, it is recommended that you also have an HDMI cable, a wide screen monitor or television with HDMI input, an Ethernet cable, and a USB keyboard.

The following table describes the main differences between the various models:

Model	Generation 2 Model B	Model B+	Model A+
Soc	BCM2836	BCM2835	
CPU	900 MHz Quad Core ARMv7	700 MHz single core ARMv6	
GPU	VideoCore IV @ 250Mhz / OpenGL ES 2.0 / H.264/MPEG-4 AVC		
SDRAM	1 GB	512 MB	256 MB
USB	4	2	1
Audio in	No direct input and two revision boards via I2S, all of which use a USB		
Network	10/100 Mbit/s		None
GPIO	17	17	17
Header	40 pins	26 pins	26 pins
Power	800 mA (4.0 W)	800 mA (4.0 W)	200 mA (1 W)
SD card	Micro SD slot		

With the latest models of the Raspberry Pi, most peripherals should work out of the box, as these versions have been upgraded with a dedicated power circuit to handle peak loads but also reduce overall power consumption. Only the plus models have this new circuit, and all the older versions of Raspberry Pi might suffer from power problems caused by inefficient circuits. The most power-efficient Raspberry Pi is Model A+ and is commonly powered using batteries. We will discuss powering your Raspberry Pi from batteries in a later chapter of this book.

Power supply

The Raspberry Pi 2 should ideally be powered using a 2 amp USB power supply if you plan to connect peripherals to the USB ports. The most common power supplies found at home are 1 amp power supplies, which are typically supplied with smartphones, tablets, or mini computers. These chargers are usually made from good quality components and can easily handle the stress of additional power, power spikes, and produce a clean DC power source, which is very important for Wi-Fi or serial peripherals.

You should also pay attention to the USB cable that you are using as some cables are produced cheaply and the copper wire inside them is very thin, which struggles to deliver 1 amp or more of current when needed.

In an independent test, the best USB charger turned out to be the HP TouchPad charger (P/N 157-10157-00), and the next best ones are Apple A1265, Apple iPad A1357, and Samsung Cube ETA0U80JBE. They are considered to be the best because they produce very clean DC power and can handle peak loads for extended periods of time. Be careful, though, as a lot of counterfeit chargers are also being sold now, especially Apple A1265. As time passes, some of these power supplies may become obsolete. Try and search for newer tests.

To help visualize the DC noise problem, examine the following image. The waveform on the left-hand side is extremely noisy and will cause serious problems for communication peripherals such as Wi-Fi, bluetooth, or even serial. The waveform on the right-hand side is considered to be clean and stable:

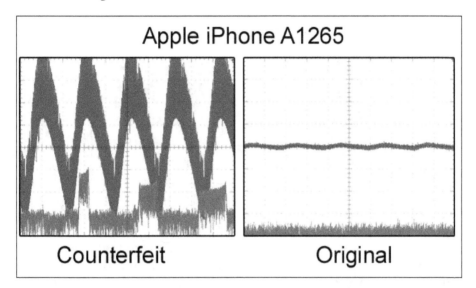

 Search the Internet for tips on how to identify counterfeit chargers.

USB hub

When you purchase a powered USB hub, it is usually supplied with a 2 or 3 amp power supply. This is enough to power USB devices such as a Wi-Fi adapter, a USB hard drive, a few other peripherals, and even the Raspberry Pi itself.

A typical problem occurs with HD USB cameras where the picture goes black after a running for some time. Using a powered USB hub will solve this problem.

SD cards

SD cards all look alike, but, in fact, some use a multitude of different controllers and NAND Flash memory chips. All these combinations make up the reliability and speed of the card; the cheapest is the worst, usually. That said, spending a fortune on an SD card is not a good idea either. The speeds of SD cards are marked with a numeric symbol ranging from 1, the slowest, to 10, the fastest. A class 6 or 8 SD card is a good balance between performance and price.

However, not all Class 10 cards are the best choice either. The only way to be sure is to use a trusted speed test application to verify that the card is performing at the advertised read and write speeds; this is the best way to identify counterfeit cards:

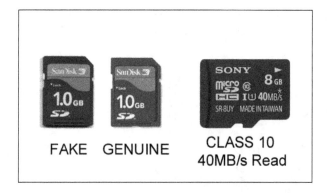

The SD card should only act as the primary partition for an operating system and applications installed on it. Using an SD card for frequently changing data, such as databases, is not a good idea as it degrades the life of the card faster than expected. Instead, we should use external storage devices, such as hard drives or **Network Attached Storage** (**NAS**), to handle frequently changing data but also help with storing large amounts of media.

This book assumes that you are using at least an 8 GB SD card.

Extra peripherals

The Raspberry Pi is branded as a computer, and it is expected that we can connect various different devices to it. Raspbian is based on Debian, and an immense effort has been made to port the majority of drivers and software available for Raspbian. You might have some old USB peripherals lying around, for example, a joystick. If you can find a driver for any other Linux platform, it should be possible to make it work with Raspbian. Plug it in, use the lsusb command-line utility, and check whether it has been detected. If you manage to get it working with your knowledge, you should share this knowledge on a forum for the benefit of other users.

Essential peripherals

You should consider buying these peripherals and dedicating them for the use of your Raspberry Pi. They will really make it easier to set everything up and are even used for long-term purposes:

- **Wireless USB network adapters**: At the time of writing this book, the current Raspbian image supports a variety of wireless adapters without the need to install any extra drivers. Many of the mini, nano, or micro versions run directly from the Pi's USB ports and do not require a powered USB hub.

- **USB hubs**: Because some versions of the Raspberry Pi are limited to two USB ports, it might be wise to have a compatible, powered USB hub. Powered is the key word here, as this will allow you to plug in any USB device or several devices at the same time without affecting the Pi's power stability. At the time of writing this, Raspbian is not fully compatible with three USB hubs yet.

- **Keyboards and mice**: Most wired keyboards and mice will run directly off the Raspberry Pi USB port. Many Bluetooth keyboards and mice also work directly off the Pi's USB ports but require initial setup using a wired keyboard. Some wireless keyboards, such as the Microsoft 3000 series, do not need any configuration as the USB dongle emulates a PS/2 wired keyboard and can be used straight away at boot time without any extra configuration.

[You can visit `http://elinux.org/RPi_VerifiedPeripherals` for an up-to-date list of compatible peripherals.]

Useful peripherals

As you grow more familiar with your Raspberry Pi, you will think of new a bigger ideas for your projects. With such ideas, you might need a few more useful devices to help you out.

Internet 3G dongles

You can connect to the Internet using a 3G dongle. These require a lot of power and will need to run from a powered hub to operate at full speed. They are a really easy way to connect your Raspberry Pi to the Internet even in the most remote places of your country. As long as you have a basic voice signal, you should always be able to use GPRS (single channel 57.5 kbps or dual channel 115 kbps), which can be enough to send plenty of logging text data. Some countries offer free text messages, and this can also be used to send and receive the bare minimum of data. If you plan to run a server, it would be recommended that you use LAN or Wi-Fi connected to an ADSL/DSL connection instead.

Audio recording

The Raspberry Pi has its own sound output hardware, which is really good at giving you a high definition sound over HDMI or analog audio via the 3.5 mm jack.

You might find yourself in a situation where you would like to record audio from a line input or microphone; you could then use any USB 1.1 or USB 2.0 sound capture device to do this.

Other media add-ons

- **IR receivers**: Infrared (IR) receivers are a great way to control your Raspberry Pi using conventional remote controls. The FLIRC USB IR remote dongle is a great way for you to start doing this.

- **TV and radio receivers**: This is the ultimate way to turn your Raspberry Pi into a full DVR system. Record, playback, or pause live TV from HD satellite or digital TV. You can listen to your favorite radio channels too.

- **Webcams**: The Raspberry Pi has a port for its own dedicated HD camera module. Owning one of these cameras is a real treat, and the latest versions of Raspbian support UV4L (Video for Linux). A variety of USB webcams are also supported and support UV4L. Once a fairly complicated task, it has now become a lot easier to work with.

- **Multicard readers**: These come in handy if you work with various card types. Support is limited on generic types, but the USB 3.0 USRobotics all-in-one card works really well, and you can mount all six cards at the same time.

- **Alamode**: WyoLum is a start-up business that creates useful add-ons for various applications. Specifically, AlaMode is an Arduino-compatible board with a real-time clock and microSD slot that sits on top of the Raspberry Pi. You can communicate with Arduino using the Pi's dedicated UART (Universal Asynchronous Receiver/Transmitter), and it can run off the Pi's power source. If you like electronic projects and are already familiar with Arduino, this is worth looking at. You can even use it to flash other Arduino-compatible chips or upload firmware to run on its own!

- **HDMI to VGA**: If you use an older or spare monitor, television, or LCD screen that only works with VGA, you can purchase an inline HDMI to VGA converter from your favorite online auction shops or electronic stores. You must make sure to buy an active converter, which is slightly more expensive than a passive convertor. Active means that it contains a microcontroller that uses power from the HDMI port to convert the digital signal into the VGA standard. The Raspberry Pi is capable of powering this type of device.

Fun peripherals

You might have some of these lying around in your gadget box. Hopefully, reading about some of these less used devices might spark some creative ideas:

- **Joysticks**: Microsoft's Xbox 360 controller works like a mouse in X using **xboxdrv**, which can be installed from the package repository. Other joysticks might need a ported driver that can be found on Internet forums.

- **USB to SATA**: You can purchase simple USB to SATA controllers that allow you to attach SATA hard drives using dedicated power supplies. The real fun begins when you use hardware RAID-based USB to SATA controllers that can be chained in various configurations, which can give you massive storage, high redundancy, or maximum performance.

 Be careful, though, as the maximum throughput speed you can achieve is governed by the bandwidth of USB 2.0. In theory, this is a maximum speed of 60 MBps, but is shared by all the devices on the controller and not per port. There is more information about this later in the book.

- **CAN bus**: The CAN bus is the standard used in all modern motor vehicles. It is a standard port that gives mandatory data that can be interpreted by anybody, for example, throttle value, misfiring of cylinders, or air to fuel ratio. PEAK-System has a variety of peripherals and software that are compatible with the Raspberry Pi. If you have access to manufacturer-specific codes, you can even adjust engine mappings with these tools.

 Adjusting non-standard values may damage your ECU and will void any warranties.

- **Home automation**: A compatible device called TellStick runs well as a third-party, home automation device for the Raspberry Pi, but as an advanced Linux user, you should strive to make your own applications using real-time microcontrollers, such as Arduino on AlaMode, or the very cheap PICAXE microcontrollers.

- **USB missile launcher**: Available on a variety of websites and stores, this is the perfect gadget if you need to shoot plushy missiles at unidentified objects! This is purely an entertainment peripheral, but you could use it for DIY projects as well.

- **Fingerprint scanners**: Futronic's fingerprint scanners work well with Raspbian, and there are many examples that can be found online. They are standalone programmable devices that communicate with the Pi using simple messages over USB-UART and have extensive documentation available with the device.

- **Weather station**: Sparkfun sell a pretty complete weather station that includes a wind vane, anemometer, and tipping bucket rain gauge. The kit includes clamps and mounting masts. You can add a light, temperature, and humidity sensor easily and without breaking the bank. The challenge depends on using a real-time microcontroller and building your own database to log all the data. But don't worry, there are many tutorials online that will help you progress further.

Installing Raspbian on the Raspberry Pi

There are many distributions that can run on the Pi. Some are specific real-time operating systems, such as RISCOS, or mainstream operating systems, such as Raspbian or Archlinux. A few flavors of home media centers, such as OpenElec or OSMC (previously known as XBMC). As of June 2015, you will also be able to install Windows 10 Internet of Things. No Android support is foreseen for the near future.

The Raspberry Pi Foundation recommends that you use their image called NOOBS (New Out Of Box Software,) which contains frequently updated list of different operating systems. In this book, we will be using Raspbian. It is supported by the Foundation and has the best compatibility with ease of use. Raspbian is based on Debian and is similar to many other Linux operating systems. The steps for installing Raspbian are as follows:

1. For Windows and Macintosh users, it is recommended by the Raspberry Pi Foundation that you use the SD Formatter from `http://www.sdcard.com`.

    For Windows, perform the following steps:

    1. Install the SD card formatting tool.
    2. Set the **Format size adjustment** option to **ON** in the **Option** menu.
    3. Make sure you've selected the correct SD card.
    4. Click on the **Format** button.

    For Macintosh, perform the following steps:

    1. Install the SD card formatting tool.
    2. Select **Overwrite Format**.

3. Make sure you've selected the correct SD card.

4. Click on the **Format** button.

For Linux, perform the following steps:

1. It is recommended that you use the GParted or Parted tool in Linux.

2. Format the entire disk as FAT.

2. You should download the latest NOOBS archive from
   `http://www.raspberrypi.org/downloads/`

3. Unzip the archive.

4. Copy the extracted files onto the formatted SD card.

5. Insert the SD card into the Raspberry Pi. Plug in your HDMI or other video cable with a compatible keyboard and power it up.

6. The Pi will boot up and present the list of operating systems; select **Raspbian**.

7. If your display is blank, try to press the numeric keys, as listed here, while the Pi is booted up:
   - *1*: HDMI mode
   - *2*: HDMI safe mode
   - *3*: Composite PAL
   - *4*: Composite NTSC

Understanding the design of the Raspberry Pi

The Raspberry Pi has two identifiable microchips on the PCB:

- In the center is one that's clearly marked with a Broadcom logo and text starting with BCM283x, which is the main processor

- The Raspberry Pi 2 has its RAM chip at the back of the PCB.

- Near the USB port, there is a smaller chip that is either a USB hub or a USB/ LAN chip, depending on the model.

BCM283x is actually a high-performance GPU with an embedded ARM processor. It is a SoC (System on Chip), which means that there is small amount of space for code that executes when it gets turned on. This is known as Stage 1 in the boot process.

Boot process

Some network actions need to be performed during the boot process, and it is good to understand the various stages in case you need to troubleshoot something. The boot process is as follows:

1. Stage 1 begins on the GPU and executes the code SoC firmware, which starts to load Stage 2 code to the L2 cache.

2. Stage 2 reads `bootcode.bin` from the SD card. It initializes SDRAM (synchronous dynamic random access memory) and loads Stage 3.

3. Stage 3 is the `loader.bin` file. This loads `start.elf`, which starts the GPU.

4. During `start.elf`, it prepares to load `kernel.img`.

5. The kernel image then reads `config.txt`, `cmdline.txt`, and `bcm283x.dtb`.

6. If the `.dtb` file exists, it is loaded at 0×100, and the kernel is loaded at 0×8000 in memory.

7. The kernel image is the first binary that runs on the ARM CPU, and it can be compiled with custom support for specific hardware.

8. The operating system starts to load.

All the source code in stages 1 to 3 are closed source and protected by Broadcom. These closed source files are compiled and released by Broadcom only; you can update them on your SD card by running a firmware upgrade in Raspbian, which is covered later.

The `kernel.img` file connects the application to the hardware. Any computer with an operating system has a kernel of some sort. In Linux, it is possible to compile your own kernel, and it might be the first file that you might want to amend yourself. This allows you to change the boot screen, load custom drivers, or perform other tasks that you might need. This is an advanced task and is not covered in this book.

Other capabilities

BCM283x also has dedicated audio hardware together with video encoding/decoding. This allows the Raspberry Pi to playback HD (MPEG-4) content, such as videos, or render games using OpenGL ES. You can buy additional encoder/decoder licenses for extra functionality, such as MPEG-2, used in DVD video encoding and VC-1, which is used by Microsoft's WMV formats. This is also used for Silverlight live streaming.

The SD card is also directly interfaced by the Broadcom chip using dedicated hardware inputs/outputs and interrupts.

All that dedicated hardware means that while those sections of the chip are fully utilized, the ARM CPU will be idle or hardly used. This allows you to compute other transactions synchronously, and this is what makes the Raspberry Pi a truly unique single board, credit card-sized computer!

Hardware limitations

All this hardware that is crammed into one tiny space has its drawbacks. Some are deliberate and others are not. You should consider that these are theoretical calculations; real-world performance may vary, but are usually slower than theoretically estimated.

Network speeds

It may be disappointing that the Raspberry Pi Foundation decided to use a 100 Mbps LAN chip instead of a gigabit one. We need to crunch some numbers to justify this decision, though. Let's convert megabits to a more familiar megabytes. To get to *megabytes per second* from *megabits per second*, we divide 100 Mbps by 8 (there are eight bits in a byte). This equates to 12.5 megabytes per second at 100% LAN capacity. For a single user, this is only roughly 20% of what the USB hub can handle. This means that by design, this is an unchangeable bandwidth limitation for networking.

If you plan to share files with several users at the same time, each new user will bump down the other user's bandwidth to accommodate their own. As a workaround, you could add a USB gigabit LAN peripheral. But due to speed constraints of the USB hub, you will only use approximately 48% of the gigabit LAN. To make matters worse, any hard drives running on the USB port will start to fight for bandwidth. The USB controller has to share 480 Mbps across all ports! One port is used by the 100 Mbit network card, and the other connects the hub to the GPU. For one user, this means a maximum bandwidth of 240 Mbps. Why 240 Mbps? This is because 240 Mbps goes to the LAN and 240 Mbps goes to the hard drive, and theoretically, there is no USB bandwidth left for anything else.

This could be a problem for a multiuser environment, but for home use, you would not run into any major problems as the bandwidth can accommodate HD video streams while serving other clients. This is why the cheaper 100 Mbps version was used.

USB bottlenecks

As it was made clear by the bottlenecks found in the LAN, the worst thing about USB bottlenecks is that there is no way to work around this problem! This is because the USB controller connects to the Broadcom and LAN chips, respectively, on the PCB without any possibility of expanding or bypassing this chip.

Time

The Raspberry Pi also does not come with a real-time clock, so timekeeping is left to Internet-based time servers. For many people, this might not cause a problem, but if you wanted to create a remote, disconnected device that depends on recording events at various times of the day, you might be left a little bit disappointed.

One easy and reliable way to do this is to connect a USB or I²C RTC that runs off a small battery. There is an easier and free option, though, but it is not as accurate; you may want to install the `fake-hwclock` package. All you need to do is set the time once, and the software will keep the track of time using a file. If you have a power outage, the software will read the file and set the time back to the last known time. The drawback is that you lose that time as there is no way to determine how long the outage lasted for.

To get time without using the Internet, you can find a cheap GPS receiver. When the GPS gets a good lock, it will provide you with extremely accurate time. This same method is used to synchronize GSM voice calls on mobile phone technologies across the world.

Another method is to use the time broadcasted by long wave radio signals. These also broadcast extremely accurate time using atomic clocks. The availability depends on your location, though. These are currently available in Colorado for most of the US; Germany, Russia, the UK for Europe; and finally, Japan. The radio waves operate on different frequencies and more research is required for this method.

References

The following are the references for this chapter:

- Visit for more information on the USB power benchmark `http://www.righto.com/2012/10/a-dozen-usb-chargers-in-lab-apple-is.html`.
- Crystal Disk Mark is a great SD card benchmarking tool with a lot of test results available online for comparison.

Summary

One of the most popular questions found on the Internet was how to increase the Pi's performance! With the release of the Generation 2, ARM V7, quad core 900 MHz, this is no longer the case. At the time of writing this book, one of the most popular questions is how to run the Raspberry Pi using batteries, which we will cover in a later chapter!

The purpose of understanding the architecture is vital to a successful long term project. The Raspberry Pi works *like* any other computer, but it was designed purely for experimental and learning purposes. It should not be used in production environments, but it is an extremely attractive solution for production nevertheless.

It is an excellent platform to share media between friends at school; it is fantastic to stream HD media on your TV and is robust enough for many standalone applications.

In the next chapter, you learn how to set up networks on the Raspberry Pi.

2

Preparing a Network

It is important to learn how your network works, especially if you plan to connect your Raspberry Pi to the Internet. A home user will typically use an Internet package designed to browse websites and read e-mails. Business packages, on the other hand, need to do a lot more than you think. These two different ISP packages usually carry important technical differences that dictate how your network can be reached.

In this chapter, you will learn how to connect to the Internet and look at how to solve some common problems for home users. You will also learn how to benchmark your network and try to isolate any network-related issues.

Local Area Network (LAN)

Using the standard Raspbian package, both essential and non-essential drivers are included. All essential drivers are loaded and some non-essential ones are as well.

We will start by plugging in a network cable between the Raspberry Pi and the router provided by your ISP. By default, your router has a DHCP server that automatically assigns an IP address to your Raspberry Pi.

You may also use network switches to make a more complex network but because the Raspberry Pi has a 100 megabit network port, it may downgrade your entire network to 100 megabits. Some switches can negotiate separate connections to lower speed interfaces without downgrading the entire network, but you need to consult the specifications of the device in order to do this.

To check whether your LAN is up and running, just type `ifconfig`, and you will get text containing your current settings:

```
eth0        Link encap:Ethernet  HWaddr b8:27:eb:45:bb:fa
            inet addr:192.168.1.135  Bcast:192.168.1.255  Mask:255.255.255.0
            inet6 addr: fe80::ba27:ebff:fe45:bbfa/64 Scope:Link
            UP BROADCAST RUNNING MULTICAST  MTU:1500  Metric:1
            RX packets:89 errors:0 dropped:0 overruns:0 frame:0
            TX packets:96 errors:0 dropped:0 overruns:0 carrier:0
            collisions:0 txqueuelen:1000
            RX bytes:7943 (7.7 KiB)  TX bytes:14104 (13.7 KiB)

lo          Link encap:Local Loopback
            inet addr:127.0.0.1  Mask:255.0.0.0
            inet6 addr: ::1/128 Scope:Host
            UP LOOPBACK RUNNING  MTU:16436  Metric:1
            RX packets:0 errors:0 dropped:0 overruns:0 frame:0
            TX packets:0 errors:0 dropped:0 overruns:0 carrier:0
            collisions:0 txqueuelen:0
            RX bytes:0 (0.0 B)  TX bytes:0 (0.0 B)
```

Let's try to understand the different keywords from the preceding output:

- **HWaddr**: This is your Pi's MAC address, which identifies a vendor and should ideally provide a globally unique address.

- **inet addr**: This is your current LAN IP address, which belongs to a private range of either `10.x.y.z` (Class A), `172.16.y.x` (Class B), or `192.168.x.x` (Class C). They are known as private addresses because they do not exist on the Internet.

- **Bcast**: This is a reserved address that's calculated by your network mask, and it transmits global messages within your private network.

- **Mask**: This is used in all networks but should only be concerned with advanced configurations. Masks divide a network into subnet works and depend on the class your network belongs to.

- **inet6 addr**: This is your IPv6 address. It will show only if your router supports this, but it is more difficult to remember.

- **RX**: This shows how many packets have been received.

- **TX**: This shows how many packets have been sent.

The eth0 port

The Raspberry Pi will typically use **eth0** as its on-board LAN interface. If you add USB LAN devices, they will have an incremented number after *eth*; this will increment the interface number.

The wlan0 interface

When we add a wireless adapter, ifconfig will represent these interfaces using wlan instead of the eth prefix. All the details are the same, but it helps to visually identify wired networks from wireless ones.

The loopback (LO) interface

This is known as the home address because it refers to the local device and has a reserved range starting from 127.0.0.1 and ending at 127.255.255.254. This is a virtual interface that bypasses local hardware interfaces and rules. It is commonly used for security reasons and during software testing. For example, you may only allow the root access of MySQL to a localhost (this will include 127.0.0.1 for IPv4 or ::1 for IPv6). This means that only the user or service on the computer will be granted access to this resource. It is reserved, and neither the localhost nor 127.x.y.z can be assigned to users on the Internet.

A wireless configuration (Wi-Fi)

Wi-Fi is a convenient way to allow your Raspberry Pi to operate in a wireless environment within a wireless network. It is not an ideal solution for servers, though, as there is an increased latency in transmitting data, and many Wi-Fi networks suffer from noise generated by other networks on the same frequency.

There are many types of wireless adapter available, and not all drivers are included with Raspbian. You might have to install a specific driver, but this is usually a simple process. When talking about wireless configuration, you have to target the chip that is used on the adapter and not the end vendor who is selling it.

Recommended wireless adapters

One of the most stable and affordable chipsets is *Realtek RT8191*, which works with the *802.11n* standard. It is also compatible with the older 802.11b/g specifications, just in case your router does not support the newer 802.11n specification. However, it does not support 5 GHz frequencies or the 40 MHz dual band.

 There is a comprehensive list of compatible adapters available at http://elinux.org/RPi_USB_Wi-Fi_Adapters.

Shop around to find the best price, and it's best to not go for overpriced adapters that claim to be the only and the best ones for your Raspberry Pi.

 You should be aware that, by default, wireless and wired networks do not work in combined mode. After configuring Wi-Fi you will need to remove your wired connection and reboot the Raspberry Pi. This will configure the wireless interface correctly. Connecting the wired connection usually drops the wireless connection after the Raspberry Pi has been booted.

Setting up from a desktop

Using the Wi-Fi configuration tool found in the menu bar while you're on the desktop is the most convenient way to connect to your wireless within seconds. It is recommended that you start with this if you have just installed Raspbian and plan on using Wi-Fi instead of an Ethernet connection. Your SSID, which is the readable name of your wireless access point, has to be broadcasted by your router for this to work. If you have it hidden, you should use the console method instead. Follow these steps to set up a desktop:

1. Left-click on the network icon found at the end of the menu bar on the right-hand side.
2. All unhidden networks will be displayed.
3. Left-click on the network you would like to connect to.
4. Enter your password and click on **OK**.
5. After a few seconds, the icon will stop flashing.
6. You can right-click on the network icon to adjust the network settings.

Setting up from a console

If you plan to run your Raspberry Pi in headless mode (where you do not have a monitor or the keyboard connected), you do not need to access the desktop by default, and you also cannot use the desktop network utility.

In the latest distributions of Raspbian, the SSH service is enabled by default, and you can SSH into your Raspberry Pi. If you have just joined your Wi-Fi network, you can tweak its settings. This is intended when you use Ethernet in order to set up the Wi-Fi. You can now log in via the SSH, and enter the following command:

```
sudo nano /etc/network/interfaces
```

This will open the included file editor, called `nano`, and present you with your current interface configuration. We are interested in the last few lines. If you do not see some of the lines, you can type them in manually:

```
auto lo

iface lo inet loopback
iface eth0 inet dhcp

allow-hotplug wlan0
auto wlan0

iface wlan0 inet dhcp
        wpa-ssid "ssid"
        wpa-psk "yourpassword"
```

To save the file, press *CTRL + X*, followed by *Y*, and finish by pressing *Enter*.

The `allow-hotplug` command will do as its name suggests: it allows you to plug wireless adapters in and out assigned to the `wlan0` interface. `Auto wlan0` tells Raspbian to configure the interface automatically based on the settings you provide.

We need to replace SSID and the password with the details of your router, keeping the text enclosed within quotation marks. This is the most basic configuration that can be used.

There is one problem with this configuration, though: if the wireless disconnects from your router, the interface will not be brought back up automatically. There are many scripts that try to solve this problem. The configuration requires that you know extra details about the wireless configuration. The next section offers a fully automatic way to do this. We will use `wpa-supplicant`, which is now installed by default with Raspbian. In `/etc/network/interfaces`, we change the last few lines to the following:

```
allow-hotplug wlan0

iface wlan0 inet manual

wpa-roam /etc/wpa_supplicant/wpa_supplicant.conf

iface default inet dhcp
```

We need to go to the `/etc/wpa_supplicant` directory, create the file, and edit `wpa_supplicant.conf`:

```
sudo touch wpa_supplication.conf

nano wpa_supplication.conf
```

Downloading the example code

You can download the example code files for this book from your account at http://www.packtpub.com. If you purchased this book elsewhere, you can visit http://www.packtpub.com/support and register to have the files e-mailed directly to you.

You can download the code files by following these steps:

- Log in or register to our website using your e-mail address and password.
- Hover the mouse pointer on the **SUPPORT** tab at the top.
- Click on **Code Downloads & Errata**.
- Enter the name of the book in the **Search** box.
- Select the book for which you're looking to download the code files.
- Choose from the drop-down menu where you purchased this book from.
- Click on **Code Download**.

You can also download the code files by clicking on the **Code Files** button on the book's webpage at the Packt Publishing website. This page can be accessed by entering the book's name in the **Search** box. Please note that you need to be logged in to your Packt account.

Once the file is downloaded, please make sure that you unzip or extract the folder using the latest version of:

- WinRAR / 7-Zip for Windows
- Zipeg / iZip / UnRarX for Mac
- 7-Zip / PeaZip for Linux

In nano, a simple text editor, we need to type the following:

```
ctrl_interface=DIR=/var/run/wpa_supplicant GROUP=netdev
update_config=1


network={
  ssid="ssid"
  proto=WPA RSN
  key_mgmt=WPA-PSK
  pairwise=CCMP TKIP
  group=CCMP TKIP
  psk="password"
}
```

The configuration file contains some extra details about the connection. The way the supplicant works is that it will try to connect using the defined parameters for `proto`, `pairwise`, and `group`. You might have to adjust `key_mgnt`, but `WPA-PSK` is the most common configuration for modern wireless routers.

This method will also allow you to connect to your router if it does not broadcast its SSID.

 It is a common misconception that disabling the SSID broadcast protects your network. There are tools that can still find SSID names using normal wireless cards without any effort, even though you have turned this off. The best security is to use the latest encryption protocol and a complex password.

Using wicd-curses

Using the `wicd-curses` package is a simpler way of setting up wireless and even wired interfaces in the console. The package allows you to edit advanced options such as a static IP, DNS, and hostnames. A daemon also runs in the background, which automatically reconnects the interface if the wireless signal drops out and is a more reliable way of maintaining a wireless network in poor signal areas. To use this package, you should comment out any settings in the `wpa_supplicant` interfaces file:

 Installing this package will install many other dependency packages and can take up in excess of 8 MB of extra space. Some sources also claim that running this daemon uses more overhead, but this sounds like a fair price to pay for ease of use and reliability, especially with Raspberry Pi 2.

```
sudo apt-get install wicd-curses
sudo wicd-curses
```

You will get a console screen with a list of available wireless access points. Use the cursor keys to select your access point, and press the right arrow key to edit its properties.

 If you see the message that no wireless networks were detected, try to open the preferences window by pressing *P*, and type wlan0 in the wireless interface field.

Once you are in the configuring preferences screen for wireless networks, you would only need to enter your password in the key field. Save the settings by pressing *F10*.

If you set up the wireless connection using a wired connection, you will need to press *C*, which will connect to the access point. Keep an eye on the status LED on your Wi-Fi (if it has one). You should see it start to flicker, and after a few seconds, it should become solid, which means a connection has been established. At this point, it is highly likely that the SSH session will be dropped because the wired connection gets disabled. You should unplug the wired connection and reconnect using the wireless IP or hostname.

 You can find the wireless IP by logging into your router via the web interface and looking at the DHCP list.

A static network address

Some DHCP servers on routers tend to change your private address every now and then. Setting a static private address is a quick way to prevent this from happening, and it is easier to remember what the IP address is.

However, many newer routers have the ability to assign a preferred IP address in the DHCP settings or will automatically assign a long-term IP to the device based on its MAC address. A long-term IP usually means that the router is reset to factory defaults or it will run out of IP addresses and replace the oldest entry in the DHCP list.

The downfall of using static addresses with most home routers is that the router might not know about this device. The reason for this is because it would have to scan the entire network endlessly, thus taking up valuable resources. If the DNS service does not advertise the IP address of the Raspberry Pi, you will not be able to use its hostname (which is, by default, `raspberry`), and instead, you will have to type in the full IP address. Furthermore, if you want to use your Raspberry Pi as a media center, it will take much longer or may even not show up in the network list. Worst of all, some routers will not allow you to forward ports to your Raspberry Pi if it is not in the DHCP client list.

It is good practice to always have a DHCP server control that's assigned IP addresses on the network so that the DNS server running beside it can work properly. Assigning a static IP address is easy with `wicd-curses`, but you could disable DHCP and DNS on your router and use your Raspberry Pi as a separate firewall, DHCP, and DNS server.

Setting up your own DHCP and DNS is not covered in this book as the topic itself could span several chapters depending on your needs.

Testing and benchmarking your network

These are essential tests that can be carried out to troubleshoot network problems. You can also use some of these advanced techniques to benchmark your network.

Basic tests

The simplest way to check whether you are connected to the Internet is to ping a remote address.

 The following tests were carried out over Wi-Fi to not only test the reliability of the Wi-Fi connection but to also achieve the best stability; it is always recommended that you use an Ethernet connection. These examples demonstrate the various bottlenecks that you may encounter when using Wi-Fi.

We can ping http://www.google.com, but we can also use shorthand and an easy-to-remember IP address, such as 8.8.8.8, which is Google's public DNS server. This IP address will resolve to the nearest Google DNS server in your area, and even if it goes down, there are many backup servers, making this a reliable test:

```
ping -c 1 google.com
ping -c 1 8.8.8.8
```

```
root@nas:~# ping -c 1 www.google.com
PING www.google.com (31.55.166.217) 56(84) bytes of data.
64 bytes from 31.55.166.217: icmp_req=1 ttl=57 time=16.7 ms

--- www.google.com ping statistics ---
1 packets transmitted, 1 received, 0% packet loss, time 0ms
rtt min/avg/max/mdev = 16.720/16.720/16.720/0.000 ms
root@nas:~#
root@nas:~#
root@nas:~# ping -c 1 8.8.8.8
PING 8.8.8.8 (8.8.8.8) 56(84) bytes of data.
64 bytes from 8.8.8.8: icmp_req=1 ttl=43 time=31.1 ms

--- 8.8.8.8 ping statistics ---
1 packets transmitted, 1 received, 0% packet loss, time 0ms
rtt min/avg/max/mdev = 31.118/31.118/31.118/0.000 ms
root@nas:~#
```

A ping can help you determine whether you have access to the Internet. You may want to check how fast you can download files to the Raspberry Pi. We will use popular website, `http://www.speedtest.com`, to help us do this directly in the command line. This can be represented in one line:

```
wget --output-document=/dev/null
   http://speedtest.wdc01.softlayer.com/downloads/test500.zip
```

My Raspberry Pi is connected to a fast wireless network connection, which is connected to a 75 megabit downstream-capable ISP. In the following screenshot, you can see that I've achieved about 4.27 megabytes. This varies greatly from site to site. The server used here is in America.

```
root@nas:~# wget --output-document=/dev/null http://speedtest.wdc01.softlayer.com/downloads/test500.zip
--2013-09-02 22:38:56--  http://speedtest.wdc01.softlayer.com/downloads/test500.zip
Resolving speedtest.wdc01.softlayer.com (speedtest.wdc01.softlayer.com)... 208.43.102.250
Connecting to speedtest.wdc01.softlayer.com (speedtest.wdc01.softlayer.com)|208.43.102.250|:80... connected.
HTTP request sent, awaiting response... 200 OK
Length: 524288000 (500M) [application/zip]
Saving to: '/dev/null'

 2% [>                                      ] 14,135,558  4.27M/s  eta 2m 21s
```

Advanced benchmarking tools

You may be a bit more serious about the performance of your network. Here are a few advanced ways to push your network to the maximum.

A speedtest application

There is a speed test application available on GitHub. It offers more advanced options than the command-line technique we used earlier as it automatically picks the nearest server and starts downloading a large file from there. The benefit of using the closest server will better demonstrate the maximum capacity of your wireless network or your ISP downstream using a wired connection.

Furthermore, the application also benchmarks your upstream bandwidth. This may be important to you if you were thinking of hosting applications for public Internet usage.

We will need to install git using aptitude's package manager. We do this by typing `apt-get` in the command line:

```
sudo apt-get install git-core
```

Follow the on-screen instruction to install the git package. Using the /tmp directory is ideal for short term applications. This directory in Raspbian is cleared out on each reboot or power failure. If you wish to keep the speed test application for future use, create a new directory in your home directory and update the path appropriately:

```
cd /tmp
git clone https://github.com/sivel/speedtest-cli.git
cd speedtest-cli
./speedtest_cli.py
```

iPerf

iPerf is a network administrator's secret tool that is included with Raspbian. It is a tool that tests a network by creating TCP and UDP streams. iPerf has client and server functionality, so it requires another computer, which known as the server. This can be another Raspberry Pi or computer that has iPerf installed on it.

This application will push the boundaries of your network interface and architecture. You can also use iPerf is to detect packet loss in a complex network, such as the Internet. If you have a virtual machine on the Internet, try installing iPerf on it and comparing the results of your local network against those found on the Internet. Let's install iPerf on the Raspberry Pi and remote computer:

```
sudo apt-get install iperf
```

The server will be listening for a connections type, so type the following:

```
iperf -s
```

The client will show you all the statistics related to the tests that are carried out:

```
iperf -c <ip address of server or domain name of public server>
```

Recommended bandwidth

A basic bandwidth of 256 kilobits of an up-and downstream is recommended for low use hosting of any kind. You can get away with 64 kilobits for personal use in the form of a basic website or the transfer of text data such as JSON.

It is standard practice for home ISP providers to supply you with a much larger downstream bandwidth, and with many countries reclassifying the Internet as a public utility, access to it should be faster and easier than before. But there is one main difference between home and business packages: it is the upstream bandwidth that matters when trying to serve content to users on the Internet. Typically, home Internet is only a fraction of the downstream, whereas businesses get a larger portion of the upstream, sometimes even equal, by purchasing Synchronous DSL (SDSL).

If you plan on using VoIP with Asterisk, a small upstream might cause terrible delays and jitters. But Asterisk comes licensed with GSM codecs that should work with an upstream bandwidth of 64 kilobits for a single call. You may purchase closed source codecs that work on much slower connections at the cost of voice quality.

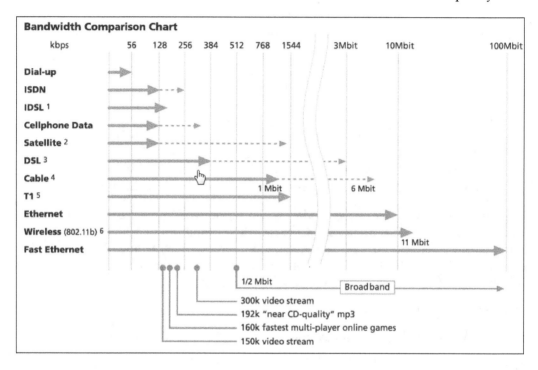

Internet configurations

There are some obstacles to resolve before you can successfully host any kind of Internet application. The solutions are influenced by the package that your ISP provides to you, but almost every problem can be worked around.

Home packages

The most fundamental part of home packages is that you almost always have a dynamic IP address. The increasing implementation of IPv6 is meant to eliminate this problem by assigning an IPv6 address to all your devices, accessible by anyone that knows it, from anywhere in the world. Some ISPs will allow you to upgrade to a static IP, but there can still be some limitations. The problem with having a dynamic IP is that it may change without notice. So, if you try to access your network from the Internet using an IP one day, it will certainly stop working after a while. This lease time varies from ISP to ISP because some are as short as a few hours, and others can last for years. If you don't know your current Internet IP address while you are in a remote place, finding out what it is can be quite inconvenient.

One of the best known solutions is to use a dynamic DNS service. Many Internet routers will have some kind of dynamic DNS setting available, even the one provided by your ISP. A dynamic DNS client is a program that automatically updates the DNS records of a public domain name. There are a handful of free dynamic DNS services.

Business packages

Business packages will almost always include a static IP address or an option to purchase one. This really gets rid a lot of work for workarounds that need to be applied with home packages. You can use the IP address provided to you, but even on the rarest occasion, it may be changed to another IP; however, you will be warned about this in advance.

The other benefits are that ISPs will allow you to change the reverse DNS lookup of your IP, a service that is unavailable with home packages. This service is very important if you plan on running a small mail server. This is one of the prerequisites that needs to be configured so that other mail domains know who you are. The only way to solve this problem at home is to use a paid for mail exchange to send and receive e-mails using custom domain names.

Many business packages offer unlimited and unshaped traffic. ISPs might deliberately throttle certain ports on home broadband connections to make them slower and less reliable. Some ISPs go to extreme measures and block these ports on home packages; for example, ports 25, 80, 110, and 443 are used for mail and web servers.

If you plan on using the Raspberry Pi for some home experiments, private use, or educational purposes, then all you need to do is spend a little extra time configuring everything correctly. Be aware, though, that hosting production services on a home broadband may be against the terms and conditions of your contract. If you anticipate high usage, it is a much better option to purchase a business package.

Dynamic DNS

Dynamic DNS is a way of updating name records for a public DNS. Paid solutions usually offer real-time updates and free services have a minimum time before the change is published.

I have been using the paid service by NO-IP, which is fairly priced for the features it provides. It also offers free domains and services. It also provides clients for many operating systems, including a Raspbian Linux-compatible client. You may use any service you like as the protocol is the same for everybody.

Installing a client

I have a premium account registered with NO-IP. I allocated a subdomain called pi.kula.solutions. It automatically detected my public IP and set the record of the domain accordingly.

 Visit http://www.mxtoolbox.com to verify live changes to domain name records. It also has several other useful tools.

Once you have created a dynamic DNS account, you can install the client on the Raspberry Pi. During the installation, you will be asked for your credentials and which domains to update.

 The make -j4 command speeds up compile time on Raspberry Raspberry Pi 2. If you are not using one, do not use -j4.

The commands to install a client are as follows:

```
mkdir /home/pi/noip
cd /home/pi/noip
wget http://www.no-ip.com/client/linux/noip-duc-linx.tar.gz
tar vzxf noip-duc-linx-tar.gz
cd noip-{version}
sudo make -j4
sudo make -j4 install
```

After running the make installation, you will be prompted to log in with your No-IP account username and password. The interval *must* be 5 minutes or more. You can now start the service:

```
sudo /usr/local/bin/noip2
```

You now have a domain name that points to your home IP address. As we progress through this book, you might want to test various applications, and to do this, you will need to open ports on your router.

Unfortunately, configuring your router is not part of this book as each vendor handles this differently. Consult the manual that came with your router to learn how to open and forward ports. Opening unnecessary ports can put you at a higher risk of being hacked.

The free Dynamic DNS domain workaround

You might not like the domain names provided by the Dynamic DNS providers, or you may not be able to afford a premium service. Instead, you may want to use a domain that you already own but is hosted somewhere else. I own another domain that is not registered with NO-IP called `http://www.piotrkula.com`. I will use this as an example to access my Raspberry Pi using `http://pi.piotrkula.com/` with a free NO-IP domain such as `http://randomname.no-ip.me`.

Log in to your domain name DNS panel, and add a new subdomain. Edit the DNS records and make sure that they have absolutely no A records associated with them. You will need to add a new CNAME record and the value; in my case, it is `randomname.no-ip.me`.

Now the `http://pi.piotrkula.com/` domain tells visitors to take a look at the `randomname.no-ip.me` DNS record instead. The visitor will find an A record at NO-IP, and this will tell them the correct IP address, which is your home IP with port 80 forwarded to the Raspberry Pi. This is *NOT* a redirect and the top domain name will *NOT* change. Visitors will not even know you are using a dynamic DNS unless they inspect your private domain record and track down that CNAME belongs to a dynamic DNS company. But as long as the domain works, there is no reason to inspect it.

The only drawback of using this workaround is speed. Whenever a visitor looks up the DNS records for the first time, it might take several seconds before a connection is established. After the first request, things go smoothly as the client usually caches the IP for the duration of the session, regardless of what TTL is set on your A record. Every new session might experience this delay as TTL forces the client to read the DNS again. Some dynamic DNS providers might even deliberately slow down DNS lookups in the hope that you will upgrade to premium DNS servers for a premium service. As far as I know, NO-IP has never done this and performed really fast, even when I used it for free domains.

Summary

It is important to understand how your networks are configured; this includes both the Internet side and your local network. This in-depth understanding will surely help you troubleshoot particular problems on your own.

We now have our Raspberry Pi connected to our private network and configured a domain name that can be accessed by anybody on the Internet.

In the next few chapters, you will learn more about various services that can be made available to friends over the Internet.

3
Configuring Extra Features

There are some extra features on the Broadcom chip that can be used out of the box or activated using extra licenses that can be purchased. Many of these features are undocumented, and are found by developers or hobbyists working on various projects for Raspberry Pi.

In this chapter, you will learn how to keep Raspberry Pi up to date and also how to use the extra features of the GPU.

Updating Raspberry Pi

The Raspberry Pi essentially has three software layers: the closed source GPU boot process, the boot loader (also known as the firmware), and the operating system. At the time of writing book, we cannot update the GPU code. But maybe, one day, Broadcom or hardware hackers will tell us how do to this.

This leaves us with the firmware and the operating system packages. Broadcom releases regular updates for the firmware as precompiled binaries to the Raspberry Pi Foundation, which then releases them to the public. The Foundation and other community members work on Raspbian, and release updates via the aptitude repository; this is where we get all our wonderful applications from.

It is essential to keep both the firmware and the packages up to date so that you can benefit from bug fixes and new or improved functionality from the Broadcom chip.

Raspberry Pi 2 uses ARMv7 as opposed to Pi 1, which uses ARMv6. It is recommended to use the latest version of the Raspbian release to benefit from the speed increase. Thanks to the upgrade to ARMv7, it now also supports the standard Debian Hard Float packages and other ARMv7 operating systems, such as Windows IoT Core.

Updating the firmware

Updating the firmware used to be quite an involved process, but thanks to a user on GitHub, who goes under by the alias *Hexxeh*, we have some code to automatically do this for us. You don't need to run this as often as `apt-update`, but if you constantly upgrade the operating system, you may need to run this if advised or if you are experiencing problems with new features or instability.

The `rpi-update` command is now included as standard in the Raspbian image, and we can simply run the following command:

```
sudo rpi-update
```

After the process is complete, you will need to restart your Raspberry Pi in order to load the new firmware.

Updating packages

Keeping Raspbian packages up to date is also very important, as many changes might work together with the fixes published in the firmware. Firstly, we will update the source list, which downloads a list of packages and their versions to the aptitude cache. Then, we will run the `upgrade` command, which will compare the packages that are already installed and also compare their dependencies, and then download and update them accordingly:

```
sudo apt-get update
sudo apt-get upgrade
```

> Updating some packages might break your existing custom code or applications if there are major changes in the libraries. If you are running custom code, you should always check the release notes if you need to change anything in your code before updating.

Updating distribution

We may find that running the firmware update process and package updates does not always solve a particular problem.

If you are using a release such as `debian-armhf`, you can use the following commands without the need to set everything up again:

```
sudo apt-get dist-upgrade
sudo apt-get install raspberrypi-ui-mods
```

Outcomes

If you have a long-term or production project that will be running independently, it is not a good idea to log in from time to time to update the packages. With Linux, it is acceptable to configure your system and let it run for long periods of time without any software maintenance. You should be aware of critical updates though, and you should evaluate if you need to install them. For example, consider the major Heartbleed vulnerability in SSH. If you had a Raspberry Pi directly connected to the public Internet, this would require instant action.

Windows users are conditioned to be updated frequently, and it is very rare that something will go wrong. But on Linux, running updates will update your software and operating system components, which could cause incompatibilities with other custom software. For example, you used an open source CMS web application to host some of your articles. It was specifically designed for PHP version x, but upgrading to version y also requires the entire CMS system to be upgraded. Sometimes, less popular open source sources may take several months before the code gets refactored to work with the latest PHP version, and consequently, they may unknowingly upgrade to the latest PHP or may partially break your CMS.

One way to try and work around this is to clone your SD card and perform the updates on one card. If you encounter any issues, you can easily go back and use the other SD card.

A distribution called CentOS tries to deal with this problem by releasing updates once a year. This is intended to make sure that everybody has enough time to test their software before you can do a full update with minimal or even no breaking changes. Unfortunately, CentOS has no ARM support, but you could follow this guideline by updating packages when you need them.

Hardware watchdog

A hardware *watchdog* is a digital clock that needs to be regularly restarted before it reaches a certain time.

Just like in the TV series Lost, there is a dead man's switch hidden on the island that needs to be pressed at regular intervals; otherwise, an unknown event will begin. In terms of the Broadcom GPU, if the switch is not pressed, it means that the system has stopped responding, and the reaction event is to restart Raspberry Pi and reload the operating system with the expectation that it will resolve the issue, at least temporarily.

Raspbian has a kernel module included — which is disabled by default — that deals with the watchdog hardware. A configurable daemon that runs on the software layer sends regular events (like pressing a button), referred to as a heartbeat to the watchdog, via the kernel module.

Enabling the watchdog and daemon

To get everything up and running, we need to do a few things, as follows:

1. Add the following in the console:

    ```
    sudo modprobe bcm2708_wdog
    sudo vi /etc/modules
    ```

2. Type the line of text bcm2708_wdog to the file. Then, save and exit by pressing *Esc* and typing :wq command.

3. Next, we need to install the daemon that will send the heartbeat signals every 10 seconds. We use chkconfig, add it to the startup process, and then enable it, as follows:

    ```
    sudo apt-get install watchdog chkconfig
    sudo chkconfig --add watchdog
    chkconfig watchdog on
    ```

4. We can now configure the daemon to do simple checks. Edit the following file:

    ```
    sudo vi /etc/watchdog.conf
    ```

5. Uncomment the lines max-load-1 = 24 and watchdog-device by removing the hash (#) character. The max load means that it will take 24 Pi's to complete the task in 1 minute. In normal usage, this should never happen and would only really occur when the Raspberry Pi has hung.

6. You can now start the watchdog with which configuration. Each time you change something, you will need to restart the watchdog:

    ```
    sudo /etc/init.d/watchdog start
    ```

There are some other examples in the configuration file that may be of interest.

Testing the watchdog

In Linux, you can easily place a function into a separate thread that runs in a new process using the & character on the command line. Exploiting this feature together with some anonymous functions, we can issue a very crude but effective system halt. This is a quick way to test whether the watchdog daemon is working correctly, and it should not be used to halt the Raspberry Pi. It is known as a fork bomb, and many operating systems are susceptible to this.

The random-looking series of characters are actually anonymous functions that create other new anonymous function. This is an endless and uncontrollable loop. It most likely adopted the name *bomb*, because once it starts, it cannot be stopped. Even if you try to kill the original thread, it creates several new threads that need to be killed. It is just impossible to stop, and eventually, it *bombs* the system into a critical state, also known as a stack overflow. Type these characters into the command line and press *Enter*:

```
: (){ :|:& };:
```

After you press *Enter*, the Raspberry Pi should restart after about 30 seconds, but it might take up to a minute.

Enabling extra decoders

The Broadcom chip actually has extra hardware for encoding and decoding a few other well-known formats. The Raspberry Pi Foundation did not include these licenses because they wanted to keep the costs down to a minimum, but they have included the H.264 license. This allows you to watch HD media on your TV, use the webcam module, or transcode media files.

They did provide a way for users to buy separate licenses if you want to use these extra encoders or decoders.

At the time of writing, the only project to use these hardware codecs was the OMXPlayer project maintained by XBMC. The latest Raspbian package has the omx package included.

Buying licenses

You can go to http://www.raspberrypi.com/license-keys/ to buy licenses, which can be used once per device. Follow the instructions on the website to get your license key.

MPEG-2

Known as H.222/H.262, it is the standard of video and audio encoding widely used by digital television, cable, and satellite TV. It is also the format used to store video and audio data on DVDs.

This means that watching DVDs from a USB DVD-ROM drive should be possible without any CPU overhead whatsoever. Unfortunately, there are no packages that use this hardware directly. But hopefully, in the near future, it will be as simple as buying this license, which will allow us to watch DVDs or stream videos in this format with ease.

VC-1

VC-1 was formally known as SMPTE 421M and was developed by Microsoft. Today, it is the official video format used in the Xbox and Silverlight framework. The format is supported by HD-DVD and Blu-ray players.

The only use for this codec would be to watch Silverlight-packaged media; its popularity has grown over the years, but it still not very popular. This codec may need to be purchased if you would like to stream videos using the Windows 10 IoT API.

Hardware monitoring

The Raspberry Pi Foundation provides a tool called vcgencmd, which gives you detailed data about various hardware used in the Raspberry Pi. This tool is updated from time to time and can be used to log the temperature of the GPU, voltage levels, processor frequencies, and so on. Some commands for monitoring are as follows:

- To see a list of supported commands, we type the following in the console:

  ```
  vcgencmd commands
  ```

- As newer versions are released, there will be more commands available here. To check the current GPU temperature, we will use the following command:

  ```
  vcgencmd measure_temp
  ```

- We can use the following command to check how RAM is split between the CPU and GPU:

  ```
  vcgencmd get_mem arm/gpu
  ```

- To check the firmware version, we can use the following command:

  ```
  vcgencmd version
  ```

The output of all these commands is a simple text that can be parsed and displayed on a website or stored in a database.

Summary

Raspberry Pi has a very capable GPU and ARM System on Chip (SOC) with features that might not have been disclosed or discovered yet. Open development is slowed down by the fact that Broadcom is keeping many aspects closed source; and even if somebody gets a peek at some source code, they enforce strict nondisclosure terms and conditions. Raspbian has had a few years to mature and many improvements have been developed since the initial release of the hardware. There is still a strong hype around Raspberry Pi, which has brought you, me, and thousands of people to this hack space.

This chapter's intention was to teach you about how hardware relies on good software, but most importantly to show you how to use leverage hardware using ready-made software packages.

In the next chapter, we will look at how to configure a web server and a database.

For reference, you can visit the following link:
`http://www.elinux.org/RPI_vcgencmd_usage`

4

Using Fast Web Servers and Databases

Raspberry Pi 2 is even better at working as a webserver now, thanks to its quad core architecture. Everything described in this chapter is still compatible with Raspberry Pi 1, but any performance tests run here are strictly for Raspberry Pi 2. The following topics will be covered in the chapter:

- Apache versus nginx versus Kestrel
- Extra frameworks for nginx
- Installing a database

Apache versus nginx versus Kestrel

With the release of .NET 5, Microsoft has managed to bring a full stack of C# deployment targets to Linux. ASP web applications, such as the popular ASP.MVC, can be hosted on Linux by using Kestrel, a development web server based on libuv. Libuv was primarily developed for use by Node.js and focuses on asynchronous input/output.

Nginx is still the first choice in embedded devices for managing HTTP traffic as an extremely fast and lightweight reverse proxy server, ahead of Apache.

Apache remains one of the more popular HTTP servers due to the fact that it comes bundled with images, but is also extremely easy to install and configure. However, it is typically used on full desktop machines or servers because it requires a lot of resources. It is not recommended to use Apache on a Raspberry Pi or other embedded device, and it will not be covered in this book.

From the Netcraft report, we can see that the three top servers are Apache, Microsoft, and nginx. Microsoft has been struggling to overtake Apache, but in August 2014, for the very first time in the last 10 years, they managed to secure the first place for a month. This was most likely caused by the fact that ASP.NET 5 was released in beta version 1 and millions of developers rushed in to test ASP.NET on Linux, Macintosh, and Windows.

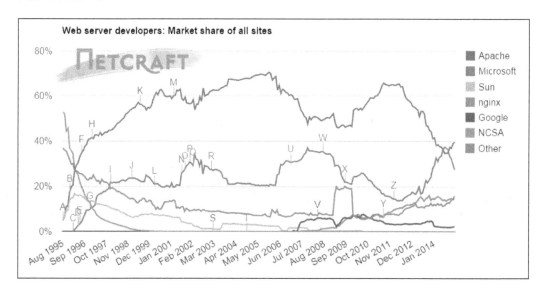

To achieve full flexibility, we will configure nginx as the frontend HTTP Proxy, which will allow us to run various combinations of programming languages in tandem. Nginx will allow us to host production-ready servers. There are almost no limits with nginx for hosting websites, and in this chapter, I will demonstrate some of the most popular ones. Nginx on its own is excellent for serving up static files, such as HTML, JavaScript, or Images.

Installing nginx

The easiest way to install nginx is to use apt-get. Unfortunately, the wheezy repository only has the version 1.2 package:

```
sudo apt-get update
sudo apt-get install nginx
```

> To upgrade to a later version of nginx, follow the instructions for selective upgrades in *Chapter 6, Setting Up Game Servers*. Then, reinstall nginx with the -t jessie switch.

By default, nginx serves pages from /usr/share/nginx/www, but most Linux admins tend to be more familiar with the location /var/www . It does not matter where you keep the files as long as you choose a convention and stick with it. We will use /var/www in this chapter:

```
sudo mkdir /var/wwww
```

Inside this directory, we will create more directories that will hold various virtual hosts. Virtual hosts are domain names (known as server blocks in nginx), which tell the webserver about the configuration for that requested domain or subdomain. We will initially create a directory called html and a directory named web that will hold static files, but will add new location blocks later, known as virtual directories:

```
sudo mkdir /var/www/html
sudo mkdir /var/www/html/web
```

Configuring the nginx virtual hosts

A virtual host in nginx is a set of rules called server blocks, which specify how to serve HTTP traffic for a specified domain. In our configuration, we will serve content to any domain on port 80. You may have many virtual hosts to serve different domains or subdomains using separate server blocks with specific domain names. This requires some more configuration and is not covered in this book.

Nginx uses the directory /etc/nginx/sites-available/ to store configuration files for virtual hosts. On starting up, it will check another directory, /etc/nginx/sites-enabled/, and usually these files are symbolic links to the configuration files in sites-available. If a file exists there, it will load the configuration file.

There should be a file called default, which is the default website that nginx serves. We will remove the symbolic link of the default website, create a new configuration file and symbolic link, and finally, restart nginx:

 We will use the symbolic name nginxhtml, but feel free to use any name you like for the virtual host.

```
sudo service nginx stop
sudo unlink /etc/nginx/sites-enabled/default
sudo touch /etc/nginx/sites-available/nginxhtml
```

Edit the configuration file found at `/etc/nginx/sites-available/nginxhtml` and add the following to it:

```
server {
  listen 80 default_server;

  location / {
    root /var/www/html/web;
    index index.html;
  }
}
```

This is the most basic configuration to serve up standard static files for any browser. This will be enough for us to use jQuery to run a client-side script, which will use AJAX requests to our APIs created later in this chapter. Let's enable the website:

```
cd /etc/nginx/sites-enabled
sudo ln -s /etc/nginx/sites-available/nginxhtml
sudo service nginx start
```

To start serving up basic pages, follow these steps:

1. Create a filename called `index.html` in the `/var/www directory`.
2. Place some basic HTML markup into it (check the code folder for a complete sample file with the jQuery download instructions and examples of calling the various APIs we will create).
3. Use a browser on another computer on your network that can access your Raspberry Pi and type the address `http://rapsberrypi` or `http://your. pi.ip.address`.
4. You should see your basic webpage now.

We should reload nginx after each configuration change by typing in the following command line:

```
service nginx reload.
```

If you get `start failed`, you can run the next command to test the configuration file, which will display any errors with details:

```
sudo nginx -c /etc/nginx/nginx.conf -t
```

Extra frameworks for nginx

Now that we have `nginx` up and running, we have a wide choice of frameworks or programming languages that we can use to create programs that will expose APIs to our basic HTML page.

We will leverage the `nginx` location blocks (virtual directories) to allow us to mix and match programming languages to deliver rich content to simple HTML pages using jQuery Java Scripting.

Python API

Python comes pre-installed with Raspbian and is the programming language of choice for Raspberry Pi. It has a rich library that allows you to access the GPIO and other system software, and there is an abundance of documentation available on the Internet.

It is an easy first language to learn, as you can create applications with fewer lines of code than in C++ or Java. You need to understand that Python is a programming language and not a web content delivery framework. This said, it is still possible to deliver web content with Python by writing specific responses. This will allow us to leverage the Python programming language to create simple APIs that can deliver data to any other software calling the API's URL.

Executing Python

You can execute any Python script in the terminal, but `nginx` cannot directly execute Python scripts. To fix this, we need to install `uWSGI`. We will configure a new location block that will ask `uWSGI` to execute Python on behalf of `nginx`, and the resulting text will be sent back to the client. We will use the latest build of `uWSGI` downloaded directly from their website. This will build and place the necessary files into the `/home/pi` directory. It should take about 80 seconds to compile on a Raspberry Pi 2:

```
cd /home/pi
sudo curl http://uwsgi.it/install | bash -s cgi /home/pi/uwsgi
```

This places the `uWSGI` binary in `/home/pi`, and we need to create a configuration file for `uWSGI` in that directory. Create a file named `uwsgi_config.ini` and enter the following text:

```
[uwsgi]
plugins = cgi
socket = 127.0.0.1:9000
chdir = /usr/lib/cgi-bin/
```

```
module = pyindex
cgi=/cgi-bin=/usr/lib/cgi-bin/
cgi-helper =.py=python
```

The actual Python script files will be located in `/usr/lib/cgi-bin` instead of `/var/www/`, as `nginx` doesn't actually execute Python files; it redirects execution to `uWSGI`. We also need to map the `nginx` location block `/cgi-bin` to `/usr/lib/cgi-bin` inside the `uWSGI` configuration file. We can now start the `uWSGI` process with the configuration. This will block your terminal; it has to run the whole time for `nginx` to be able to communicate with the daemon. Open a new terminal or run it in `screen`:

cd /home/pi

sudo ./uwsgi ./uwsgi_config.ini

Next, we will add a new location block for our default server that is purely for Python's execution. This new location block is also known as a virtual directory, where every request on the location `http://raspberrypi/cgi-bin` will actually ask `uWSGI` to execute Python files in the `/usr/lib/cgi-bin` directory.

Add the following location block under the previous location block in the existing `nginxhtml` file:

```
location / {
    include uwsgi_params;
    uwsgi_modifier1 9;
    uwsgi_pass 127.0.0.1:9000;
}
```

In `/usr/lib/cgi-bin`, we will create a file called `temp.py` that will simply return an HTTP header for the browser and the CPU temperature as text. Indentation is important here as it defines the function block:

```
#!/usr/bin/env python
import os
# Return CPU temperature as a character string
def getCPUtemperature():
    res = os.popen('vcgencmd measure_temp').readline()
    return(res.replace("temp=","").replace("'C\n",""))

#We have to print a valid HTTP header first so the browser
#will know how to decode the data
print "Content-type: text/html\n\n"
temp1=float(getCPUtemperature())
print temp1
```

One last thing we need to do is make the Python script executable:

```
chmod +x temp.py
```

If you reload the webpage that uses the sample code provided, you should now you can see the Raspberry Pi's temperature refreshed every second in the Python paragraph. You can also test it by navigating your browser to http://rasbperrypi/cgi-bin/temp.py.

This is an extremely basic sample of how you could provide data from Python in a Web API way. This is not a standard Web API JSON/XML implementation, but it is extremely lightweight and fast and an easy way to provide data via HTTP requests.

Node.js

Node.js is a platform built on the Google V8 JavaScript engine that uses event-driven and non-blocking I/O.

It is known as the JavaScript web programming language. On the surface, this is true, but deep inside Node.js binary, it uses C/C++ to access the local system resources, and then standard modules written in JavaScript (file system, networking buffering, cryptography, data streams, and so on) expose APIs from which you can then extend your own application with. You will never actually need to write any C/C++, and all the packages are provided as JavaScript; this is why Node.js is so easy to use and dubbed the JavaScript programming language.

It is a great runtime environment for Raspberry Pi because it is extremely lightweight on resources but optimized to handle hundreds of requests across many node applications.

Installing Node.js

We will use an auto setup script for Node.js. Execute the following command:

```
curl -sL https://deb.nodesource.com/setup | sudo bash -
```

We can now install Node.js from the new repository.

```
sudo apt-get install nodejs
```

Node.js and NPM are now installed. To check whether Node.js is installed correctly, you can execute the following command:

```
node --version
npm -version
```

What is NPM

NPM stands for **Node Package Manager**. You can find many ready to use applications and libraries at `http://www.npmjs.com`. These are ready to be installed with a single command line, which is provided at the packages' landing page.

Try and search for Raspberry on the website to find some interesting packages made specifically for Raspberry Pi.

The Node.js server

Typically, you would execute Node.js files using `nodejs helloword.js` and that would run the program without any web capabilities. In order for us to use Node JS in a Web API way, we need to create a Node HTTP server, which can then react to your Web Requests proxied via Nginx.

As with all the examples, we want nginx to be able to provide a standard and easy way to proxy web requests via port 80 into Raspberry Pi's internally running applications. This makes it easy to remember URLs and simpler to build frontend pages and offer some security if you are going to open your Raspberry Pi to the World Wide Web.

We will add a new location block to the existing file in the `/etc/sites-available/nginxhtml` directory:

You can run multiple node applications like this by creating new location block names (virtual directories) and adjusting the proxy pass setting that your node application is bound to.

```
location /node {
    proxy_set_header X-Forwarded-For $proxy_add_x_forwarded_for;
    proxy_set_header Host $http_host;
    proxy_set_header X-NginX-Proxy true;
    proxy_pass http://127.0.0.1:5000;
    proxy_redirect off;
}
```

We will install two packages to help get Raspberry Pi's voltage settings. Firstly, we will install a package called **express**, which will allow us to easily create RESTful APIs, and then a pi-volts module.

The typical approach with packages is to install them in your application directory, which is saved in /node_modules and is only accessible by that application. We will use the -g switch, which will install the package once into the /usr/lib/node_modules/ directory, which will be available globally to any node application you create. This saves some space on your SD card, but it means that all your applications using that global package must use that one specific version of the package. You can, however, install packages, such as express globally, and then install a small package for just one application, such as pi-volts.

Whenever you create a new application directory, you must use npm to initialize the application. This creates a configuration file and lets Node.js know that you want to install your application-specific packages (non-global) into this directory. A few onscreen questions will be displayed; you can just press **Enter** on all the questions if you like. Because nginx does not execute or serve up the raw Node.js files, we will keep our naming convention similar to Python. I will demonstrate this approach in the next few command lines:

```
sudo npm install express -g
cd /usr/lib
sudo mkdir node_bin
cd node_bin
sudo mkdir volts
cd volts
npm init
sudo npm install pi-volts
touch index.js
```

You have now set up the basic framework for your application and installed the pi-volts package just for this Node.js application. Edit index.js and insert the following text:

```
var http = require('http');
var express = require('express');
var app = express();
var volt = require("pi-volts");

// Express route for incoming requests (GET)
app.get('/node/core/voltage/', function(req, res) {
    res.send(String(volts));
});

// configure Express to listen on port 5000
app.listen(5000);
```

We can now run this basic node server, which provides a simple API text response with the current core CPU voltage. You can do a AJAX GET request at `http://raspberrypi/node/core/voltage`, and since this is a GET, you can simply test it by entering this address into your browser after starting the server:

`npm index.js`

Now, you can update your `index.html` file at `/var/www/html/web` and use jQuery to do a simple GET and update an element on your page. The result varies between 1.2 and 1.3125 (the full sample is provided in the code library):

```
$.get('/node/core/voltage', function(data) {
  $('#cpuvoltage').text(data);
});
```

.NET and ASP.MVC

To work with Microsoft's .NET framework, we first need to install the latest version of Mono. The typical way is to compile Mono from the GIt source, but it takes roughly 6 hours to complete on Raspberry Pi 2. I have tried to come up with a cross-compiling tutorial, but I have not managed to get anything simple or robust enough to demonstrate in this book.

Unfortunately, at the time, the Wheezy and Jessie repositories only have versions that do not support .NET 5 fully. A faster and better way is to use the newer versions maintained by the official Xamarin repository.

These commands will add the official Xamarin repository, update any required packages, and finally, install Mono, which requires about 300 MB of space and takes about 10 minutes to complete. Type in the following commands:

```
sudo apt-key adv --keyserver keyserver.ubuntu.com --recv-keys
3FA7E0328081BFF6A14DA29AA6A19B38D3D831EF


echo "deb http://download.mono-project.com/repo/debian wheezy main" |
sudo tee /etc/apt/sources.list.d/mono-xamarin.list


sudo apt-get update && sudo apt-get upgrade


sudo apt-get install mono-complete
```

Prerequisites for .NET 5

 Please be aware that the terminology and commands may change as the .NET vNext project leads up to version 1. If any commands do not work, please refer to `https://github.com/aspnet/home` for more information.

At this point, we can check that Mono has been properly installed by typing in the following command:

```
mono --version
```

For Kestrel to work properly, we need to compile `Libuv` and link the new libraries manually:

```
sudo apt-get install automake libtool curl unzip
wget https://github.com/libuv/libuv/archive/v1.4.2.tar.gz
sudo tar zxfv v1.4.2.tar.gz -C /usr/local/src
cd /usr/local/src/libuv-1.4.2
sudo sh autogen.sh
sudo ./configure
sudo make
sudo make install
sudo ldconfig
```

.NET 5 for Linux comes with some new terminology, which I will try my best to explain:

DNX is short for **Dot Net Execution Environment** and is used to bootstrap and execute .NET applications. To install DNX, we first need to install DNVM, which stands for **Dot Net Version Manager**.

DNVM allows you to install various versions of DNX side by side as a way to allow applications to run on various versions of .NET 5.

DNU, which stands for **Dot Net Package Updater**, essentially provides a way to restore NuGet packages on Pi on which the project depends, similar to Node.js NPM.

Installing DNVM, DNU and DNX

DNVM, DNU, and DNX can be installed using a one-line command on the terminal thanks to a script that will execute all the other required operations. Please note that the stable uses old command lines: K, KRE, KPM, and KVM. To stay up to date with patches, we will use the dev (bleeding edge) branch. These patches remove a lot of extra commands that will not be covered here. As soon as version 1 is released, please use the stable branch:

```
cd /home/pi
curl -sSL https://raw.githubusercontent.com/aspnet/Home/dev/dnvminstall.
sh | DNX_BRANCH=dev sh && source /home/pi/.dnx/dnvm/dnvm.sh
```

Installing DNX

To install the latest version of DNX (.NET 5), which as of writing is Beta4, on the dev, we can now just type in the following one-line command:

```
dnvm upgrade
```

```
dnx
```

Congratulations, you now have .NET 5 installed on your Raspberry Pi!

Running the MVC website

During the previous process, only the .NET 5 runtime environment was installed, which allowed for cross-platform execution of the .NET applications.

To get a quick MVC website running, we will use the examples from the ASPNET Github repository. During beta, please make sure you select the correct directory of the DNX version that was installed. In the rest of this chapter, we be using the v1.0.0-beta4 directories and DNX. When the final is released, it will be known as v1.0.0.

 Please double-check the DNX version and the sample version you are using. A mismatched DNX and sample will result in some of the samples failing to run.

We will clone the main APSNET Home Sample and change into the specific beta directory. We will run a package restore in this directory to install all the required dependencies, such as Kestrel:

DNU restore might take some time to download the required packages for the first time. The dnx . kestrel command might also take some time for the first time; it will bootstraps and prebuild the MVC website before Kestrel launches and binds to a port.

```
cd /var/www
sudo mkdir dotnet
cd dotnet
sudo git clone -b dev https://github.com/aspnet/Home.git
```

The Git clone was executed as the root user, creating all the files in the /Home directory as the root. This will cause a problem while restoring packages and other strange things may happen. We need to change the user recursively to pi on this directory to fix permission problems:

```
sudo chown -R pi /var/www/dotnet/Home
```

We will now restore the required packages from the official stable repository. You always need to run this on any new (or sample) project, but it will be a lot faster, since the packages are now cached (replace the beta with the DNX version you are running):

```
cd /Home/samples/v1.0.0-beta4/ HelloMVC
dnu restore
dnx . kestrel
```

The last command uses dnx to launch the MVC website using the configuration specified in the configuration file named project.json. The port to which Kestrel binds is also defined in the project.json file and is 5004 by default.

After running dnx . kestrel, your terminal screen will be blocked and will show some messages generated by .NET. Once the server has started, a message will be displayed telling you that it has started and which port it is bound to. A blinking underscore will be visible, until you press *Enter* to terminate the server.

Before you press *Enter*, use a web browser on another computer on your network and navigate to htttp://raspberrypi:5004. You should now see a basic MVC example website.

Go ahead and try to compile the other samples or create your own project using the Visual Studio Community edition.

MVC and nginx

You may use MVC as it is with Kestrel without installing nginx, but it is strongly recommended to use nginx as the frontend proxy, which will allow you to manage various web applications in a mixed environment. Nginx also provides you with more functionality, such as binding SSL certificates, which Kestrel on its own doesn't support yet.

We can now add another location block for the dotnet proxy:

```
location /dotnet {
    proxy_pass http://127.0.0.1:5004;
}
```

You can now navigate your browser to http://raspberrypi/dotnet and you should see the same page as on port 5004.

The benefit of doing this is that you have now configured nginx to do more advanced things with this virtual host.

For security reasons, you should only allow ports forwarded to the ports defined in your nginx virtual hosts and block the rest, for example, Kestrel's 5004. This is to ensure that any vulnerabilities within Kestrel cannot be exploited, while it's still developed as a development server. The only downside is that services such as Netcraft will identify this website as nginx and not Microsoft's Kestrel. But from a security point of view, this is good, since a potential attacker will not know what is actually going on behind the powerful nginx proxy.

Other .NET applications

Mono supports the full .NET 5 stack, which means that you can now easily create console applications in Visual Studio and execute them on Raspberry Pi. Simple copy your .exe file and run it using MONO file.exe.

You can also create traditional Windows Forms and execute them within LXDE using the same method of MONO formsapp.exe. Native styled forms should appear within LXDE.

With Windows IoT installed as your operating system, you will be able to create Universal Apps leveraging the Windows 10 API, creating full hardware rendered forms, and gain access to OpenGL via DirectX graphics and a rich API for developing Internet of Things applications for Raspberry Pi 2. The basics will be covered in *Chapter 10, Windows IoT Core*.

Installing PHP

As mentioned before, nginx is a proxy that handles web requests extremely quickly, and to get PHP to work with nginx, we need to install an interface called **FastCGI**. This will allow nginx to send requests to PHP and receive and display the response. To help improve PHP performance, we will also install a PHP extension called APC, which stands for **Alternative PHP Cache**. It is much faster and uses fewer resources than the standard PHP caching.

After installing, PHP should be running, but we will restart it to make sure all the extensions were loaded correctly:

```
sudo apt-get install php5-fpm php-apc
sudo service php5-fpm restart
```

Create a new directory under /var/www/ called PHP with a subdirectory web. In the web directory, we will create a new file called index.php and add the following content:

```php
<?php
    phpinfo();
?>
```

This time we will run it on a different port, as PHP has different requirements. We will bind the new host to port 888. We will create a new server block; you can place it in the existing configuration file or create a new sites-available/php file if you wish:

> Please avoid using port 8080, as it will be used for real-time streaming later.
>
> Note the fastcgi_pass setting that will be used for any other PHP website.

```
server {
    listen 888;
    root /var/www/php/web;
    index index.php;

    location ~ \.php$ {
        fastcgi_pass unix:/var/run/php5-fpm.sock;
        fastcgi_index index.php;
        include fastcgi_params;
    }
}
```

Restart nginx, and then with a browser on another computer, browse to `http://raspberrypi:888`. You should be presented with a page that looks as follows:

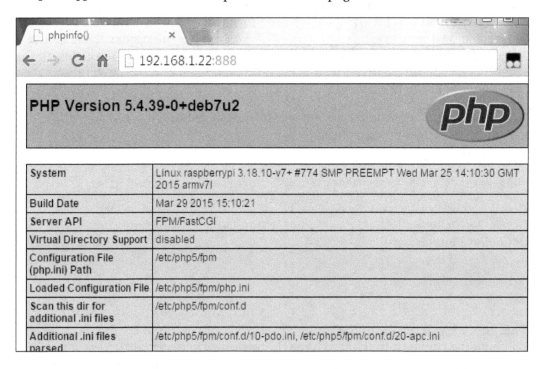

Installing a database

When we think of a database on a Linux machine, the first thing that often comes to our mind is MySQL. It is the first choice because it is free, open source, reliable, and comes with a rich toolset. On Raspberry Pi 2 with quad cores, MySQL has become an even more attractive solution, but I will still cover the alternative to SQLite that is lightweight and robust.

Installing MySQL

MySQL has been around for a very long time, and unless you are looking for a specific version, you can use the current repository to install MySQL version 5.5:

```
sudo apt-get update
sudo apt-get install mysql-server
```

You will be presented with blue-background screens asking you for the root user password. You should write these down and keep them in a secure location, but it is more convenient and secure to store passwords in an application such as `KeePass`.

 It is good practice to never use the root user with MySQL for web applications, especially the production ones available on the Internet.

Installing phpMyAdmin

A very popular SQL management tool called `phpMyAdmin` can be installed and used to further manage your databases and even transact against them.

The `phpMyAdmin` is the only application that needs to run with root settings so that it can fully manage MySQL. The best practice for `phpMyAdmin` is to only allow local network connections for administration or via SSH. This is because it will be used to create or delete databases, users, and passwords, and apply permission access to these databases. You can create less privileged users to log in via the Internet if you need too:

```
sudo apt-get install phpMyAdmin
```

During installation, you will get another blue screen asking for the web server that should be automatically configured. Regrettably, `nginx` is *not* on the list; do not check any box and click on **OK**. After a short while, a final screen will ask about `dbconfig-common`; click on **NO**.

We need to manually configure phpMyAdmin just like any other website for nginx. PhpMyAdmin places its files in the shared location `/usr/share/phpmyadmin`, and anyone with access to the system can use this shared website to access only their database.

In `sites-available`, create a new file called `phpmyadmin`; now use the following configuration. Remember to create a symbolic link in `sites-enabled` and then reload nginx:

```
server {
 location /phpmyadmin {
  root /usr/share/;
  index index.php;
  location ~ ^/phpmyadmin/(.+\.php)$ {
   try_files $uri =404;
   root /usr/share/;
   fastcgi_pass unix:/var/run/php5-fpm.sock;
   fastcgi_index index.php;
```

```
        fastcgi_param SCRIPT_FILENAME $document_root$fastcgi_script_name;
        include /etc/nginx/fastcgi_params;
    }
  location ~* ^/phpmyadmin/(.+\.(jpg|jpeg|gif|css|png|js|ico|html|xml|
txt))$
    {
      root /usr/share/;
    }
  }
  location /phpMyAdmin {
  rewrite ^/* /phpmyadmin last;
  }
}
```

This virtual host is configured to run on port 80, but in a virtual directory. The application in this virtual directory runs on its own thread, separate from anything else running on port 80. You can configure the previous virtual hosts to run in the same way if you prefer this over different port numbers.

You can now browse to `http://raspberrypi/phpmyadmin/setup` and follow the onscreen instructions. You can ignore the message about the *config* directory for now. You will need your MySQL root database password. In the servers section, click new on the **Server** button and enter the password for root under the **Authentication** tab.

 Follow the guides on screen to get the most up-to-date versions and information on the best practice.

Once you are complete, you can navigate your browser to the virtual directory, `http://raspberrypi/phpmyadmin`, and log in with your root credentials. The first thing you should do is set up a new user.

Installing SQLite

SQLite3 is a self-contained, easy-to-install, lightweight transactional database. The product's website boasts that it is the most deployed database in the world. As we know from Wikipedia, it is actually the most deployed database on embedded devices, which still leaves MySQL as the most used database. None of this really matters to us because both these databases are very good at what they do, except that SQLite is a better choice if you are looking for much better performance on your Raspberry Pi 1:

```
sudo apt-get install sqlite3 php5-sqlite
```

We will be using `phpliteadmin`, a single-file administration utility made specifically for SQLite versions 2 and 3. Also, create a new subdirectory for `phpliteadmin`. Note that the Google code is closing and the package may be moved to GitHub soon. You can search the Internet if the link doesn't resolve:

```
sudo mkdir /var/www/phpliteadmin/
sudo mkdir /var/www/phpliteadmin/web
cd /var/www/phpliteadmin/web
wget https://phpliteadmin.googlecode.com/files/phpliteAdmin_v1-9-5.zip
sudo unzip phpliteAdmin_v1-9-5.zip
```

The easiest way to get `phpliteadmin` working locally is by running it on its own dedicated port.

Create a new virtual host file `sqladmin` with the following content:

```
server
{
  listen 81;

  root /var/www/phpliteadmin/web/;
  index phpliteadmin.php;
  location ~ \.php$
  {
    fastcgi_pass    unix:/var/run/php5-fpm.sock;
    fastcgi_index   phpliteadmin.php;
    include         fastcgi_params;
  }
}
```

Reload nginx and navigate to `http://raspberrypi:81`. The default password is `admin`. At this point, you will get an error message saying that there are no databases and the directory is not writeable.

SQLite creates flat files that contain all the data, and you can manage where you would like to keep these files. There is no server managing these files, and any SQLite-compatible client can connect to these files.

You can create a test database in /var/www/phpliteadmin/web using the SQLite3 command line:

```
sudo sqlite3 test.db
BEGIN;
CREATE TABLE temps (theDate DATE, name TEXT);
COMMIT;
.exit
```

Refresh the web page where you navigated to `phpliteadmin`. You will see a new layout with a list of databases on the left-hand side. If you made the directory writeable, you can also create new databases.

> It is highly recommended not to allow access to this virtual website from the Internet as there are no security features implemented.

Summary

In this chapter, we covered how to create various basic websites running on .NET or PHP hosting platforms. Nginx is truly a versatile and fast proxy server, which helps us achieve the variety of web applications that we can provide.

We had a look at how to host .NET MVC and PHP as well as install two different types of database engines, all running side by side in harmony.

In the next chapter, we will set up file sharing for your local network and *ownCloud* for Internet-based storage.

5
Setting Up the Raspberry Pi as a File Server

Windows, Linux, and Mac OS X all use different file systems, and they have different ways of sharing files across a network. On top of all this, you also get network-specific protocols, for example, the ones that are used over the Internet.

If you are wondering which the best one is, you will never find the answer; instead, you should use the technologies that you find most suitable for your application and with which you are most familiar.

Connecting the external storage

The Raspberry Pi does not have a SATA interface, and the only way to connect this storage is by using USB ports. You can further expand the amount of USB ports by attaching a powered USB hub.

Due to the 480 MBps limitation on the USB bus, we should consider the most optimal setup. We reserve 100 MBps for Ethernet, which should be more than enough to stream any kind of HD video. This leaves us with 380 Mbps (47 MBps), which is fine because we can only send a maximum of 12 MBps of data via Ethernet anyway.

If you really want to squeeze out more transfer speed, you can use a compatible 802.11n or 802.11ac wireless USB peripheral. You may achieve in excess 100 MBps with WiFi, but there is the extra process of making sure your signal is good and that your general environment is not occupied by any other wireless router. The most optimistic transfer speed you can expect is about 25-30 MBps.

Preparing the storage medium

At this stage, it is a very good idea to use an externally-powered USB hub. USB-attached hard drives will need this extra power to operate properly. If you are using a wireless adapter and any other USB peripheral, you should consider moving them over to the powered USB hub.

 Make sure that you are not using a drive with important files. This chapter will show you how to format drives and use other file systems. All the data on your drives will be lost.

For simplicity, in this chapter, we will be using an 8 GB USB flash drive; but the concept is the same for USB hard drives.

Listing the available drives

In the console, you can use the fdisk command to get a list of drives, and partitions as shown in the following command line:

```
sudo fdisk -l
```

The fdisk command will show you the names of the disks used in Linux, their full sizes, and partitions. The drive under /dev/mmcblk is the internal SD card, and you do not want to do anything with this device. Instead, you should always look for drives marked /dev/sdxn, where *x* is usually an letter representing a physical drive and *n* is a number representing the partitions of the device in ascending order.

Unfortunately, device names are not assigned in any particular order, and there is no guarantee that the same name will be used for the same drive. This can become a problem when you start to use two or more hard drives. The partition numbers never change, though, and they represent the exact order in which the partitions were created.

The following screenshot shows that the USB flash drive has come up as the /dev/sda device, and it has 7803 MB with a FAT32 file system:

```
root@raspberrypi:~# fdisk -l

Disk /dev/mmcblk0: 3904 MB, 3904897024 bytes
4 heads, 16 sectors/track, 119168 cylinders, total 7626752 sectors
Units = sectors of 1 * 512 = 512 bytes
Sector size (logical/physical): 512 bytes / 512 bytes
I/O size (minimum/optimal): 512 bytes / 512 bytes
Disk identifier: 0x000c7b31

        Device Boot      Start         End      Blocks   Id  System
/dev/mmcblk0p1            8192      122879       57344    c  W95 FAT32 (LBA)
/dev/mmcblk0p2          122880     7626751     3751936   83  Linux

Disk /dev/sda: 7803 MB, 7803174912 bytes
122 heads, 58 sectors/track, 2153 cylinders, total 15240576 sectors
Units = sectors of 1 * 512 = 512 bytes
Sector size (logical/physical): 512 bytes / 512 bytes
I/O size (minimum/optimal): 512 bytes / 512 bytes
Disk identifier: 0xc3072e18

    Device Boot      Start         End      Blocks   Id  System
/dev/sda1    *        8064    15240575     7616256    b  W95 FAT32
```

Formatting a drive

The Raspberry Pi is capable of reading and writing to NTFS, which Windows uses. It can also read/write HFS+, which is used by Macintosh. Both these methods are fine for the temporary attachment of removable media if you need to copy something quickly.

The NTFS and HFS+ file systems are not native to Linux, and they take a lot of overhead to convert data between what Linux understands and what the other file systems understand. Some unexpected errors might occur and cause loss of data, which nobody wants!

Ext4 is the preferred storage file system in Linux. Media mounted using this file system in Linux is really fast and reliable. There are ways to use it on Mac OS X and Windows, but this is not the goal of this chapter. You should commit to using the media as long-term storage that will stay connected to the Raspberry Pi.

We first need to prepare hard drives by wiping them back to a clean state.

A word of warning is that this step will destroy all data on the target drive.

This command will quickly remove everything from your hard drive, including partitions and boot sectors. Be sure to use the correct device name that you saw in `fdisk`. In this case, it is sda, but you need to double check this on your Raspberry Pi as it maybe different. This can be done using the following command:

```
sudo dd if=/dev/zero of=/dev/sda bs=512 count=1
```

Creating a EXT4 partition

We will create a new partition using `fdisk`. I want to use the entire drive and defaults that `fdisk` provides. You can use the `m` command in `fdisk` at any time for more help, as shown in the following command-line snippet:

```
sudo fdisk /dev/sda
n "new partition"
<enter> "Uses p as the default"
<enter> "Uses 1 as the default"
<enter> "Uses default first sector"
<enter> "Uses last sector available on drive"
w "write partition data and exit"
```

The last command that we will issue is used to create the EXT4 file system on the partition on sda1. The `-L` flag in the following command line provides the name of the partition. You can use any short name that you like:

```
sudo mkfs.ext4 /dev/sda1 -L nas001
```

Mounting the drives

Linux has a directory called `/mnt` where you can create mount points for various hard drives or other network connections. There is also a directory called `/media` where you can mount drives. This is a convention used throughout Linux so that people have an idea of how to organize all these files. These are just normal directories; and if you wish, you can create your own directory called `/nas`, and you can mount all your drives associated with **Network Attached Storage (NAS)** there.

I will create a directory called `/nas` and mount my USB drive here. Then, I will create a subdirectory called `USB001`. We will also create directories that we will use for sharing, as shown in the following command-line snippet:

```
sudo mkdir /nas
cd /nas
sudo mkdir USB001
```

```
sudo mount -t ext4 -v /dev/sda1 /nas/USB001/
cd USB001
sudo mkdir public
sudo mkdir work
```

Remounting a disk after reboot

The quickest way to get your drives remounted after a reboot is to add a few lines to the fstab file, which controls the file system configuration and can be found at /etc/fstab.

Simply add the following lines. The first part is the partition, and the latter part is the mount point. You need to adjust these into your hardware. The final options are used for automounting. Do not change these options:

```
/dev/sda1 /media/USB001 auto noatime 0 0
```

Accessing files

We will go over several ways of allowing access to files on the Raspberry Pi, the network, and the Internet. You should choose the method that suits you best, as enabling more than one way makes it easier to compromise your system over the network.

The FTP service

The File Transfer Protocol specification was originally published in 1971, but we currently use a specification from 1985 that everybody should really start moving away from. FTP uses port 21.

A much newer specification, known as Secure FTP (SFTP), supports the IPv6 and Secure Socket Layer (SSL) encryption. Installing FTP will just be a waste of time as OpenSSL (SSH) comes with built-in support and is enabled by default to use SFTP. SFTP generally uses port 22, which is the same port as SSH.

You should create and use a separate user for the SFTP access. I will demonstrate how to connect to your Raspberry Pi with two popular clients using the root account for simplicity.

Connecting with FileZilla

FileZilla is open source and can be run on Windows, Mac OS X, or Linux. Download and install it on your computer. We connect to the Raspberry Pi using the following steps:

1. In the **Host** field, enter the IP address or the DNS name of your Pi;

2. In the **Username** field, enter the name of the user on the Pi. For example, `root`.

3. In the **Password** field, enter the password of this user.

4. In the **Port** field, enter the name of the port as `22`. This tells FileZilla that you want to connect using SFTP.

The following screenshot will show how FileZilla is connected to our Pi:

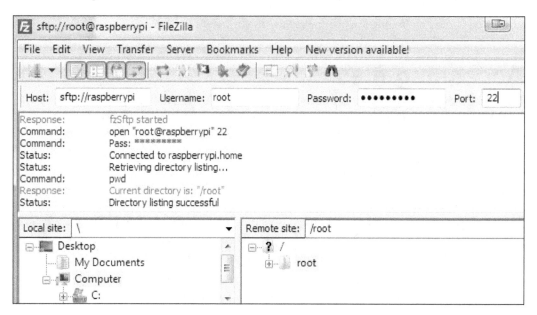

Connecting with WinSCP

WinSCP is the client preferred by all Windows users who need to connect to any Linux box running the SSH or SFTP server.

WinSCP also offers **Secure Copy Protocol (SCP)**, which is not specified by any standard. It uses Secure Shell for data transfers and the same authentication method.

Go to `http://winscp.net/` and find the [Go to **Download** page] link from where you will get the installer or portable binary.

Just like with FileZilla, you will enter the hostname, username, and password. You can use SFTP or SCP as shown in the following screenshot:

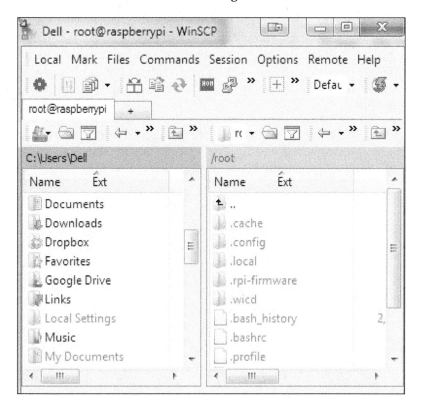

The Samba service

Samba is an implementation of the SMB/CIFS networking protocol, which is mostly used on computers running Microsoft Windows. It is basically a way of allowing a Windows computer to connect to Linux systems and access their shared files or printers. It is not created by Windows and was originally developed by Andrew Tridgell.

If you want to share media from Linux with other Windows computers on your network, Samba is the best software option.

Installing and configuring Samba

You need to install Samba and a common library that is used by Samba using the following command line:

```
sudo apt-get install samba samba-common-bin
```

You can then navigate to /etc/samba and edit the smb.conf file. On a private network for personal use, you may skip any step that requires the use of passwords to mount network shares. In an exposed or production environment, always use authentication.

If you do not like to put security on internal network shares, then this is perfectly safe. Since these files cannot be accessed from the Internet, you may just want to browse your network freely and copy or move files around without the extra pain of entering passwords.

By default, Samba is set for anonymous (unauthenticated) access. To change this, scroll down and uncomment the security = user line by removing the preceding #. This will tell Samba to authenticate against the users that you have created.

We will quickly create a user for the purpose of demonstration as there is an extra step required to add the user to the Samba authentication list. The following command-line snippet is an example of creating a system user to access Samba:

```
sudo useradd bond007 -m -G users
sudo passwd bond007
sudo smbpasswd -a bond007
```

Network shares

At the bottom of the smb.conf file, we will add two shares, as shown in the following command-line snippet. One account is for guests without authentication, whereas the other account will only be accessible by our new user—James Bond:

```
[public] comment = Media share
path = /nas/USB001/public
force user = "root"
read only = no
guest ok = yes
public = yes

[work]
comment = Work share
path = /nas/USB001/work
valid users = "bond007" #or @users to allow the group users access
force group = users
read only = no
writeable = yes
```

Samba can be quite difficult to understand in terms of permissions. Let's start off with the public share. You will notice that we put a line in `smb.conf` that says `force user = "root"`. We do this because we created the public directory as root user, so the permissions applied to the directory and all the files to be created later can only be for the user root! So, we tell Samba to imitate guests, as root, so that they can read/write as the root user.

The same will apply for the user James Bond and his directory. If you have created the work directory as the root user or Raspberry Pi, even James Bond will not be allowed to write new files. To overcome this problem, you can simply change the owner of the folder by typing the following command line:

```
chown bond007:users /mnt/USB001/work
```

You can also assign a directory to an entire group by replacing `bond007` with `users`. The command will look like `chown users:users`. This means that anybody in the group can write and delete files on this folder now.

The configuration file has many advanced features, and I recommend reading the online manual to learn more about security, sharing printers, and even how to get Samba to act like a Windows domain server!

You can now use any Windows computer to browse the network and access the newly created shares.

AFP for Macintosh

Samba also works with Macintosh, but Apple has its own networking protocol called **Apple Filing Protocol (AFP)**. There is software that you can install on the Raspberry Pi so that your Macintosh computers can detect the Raspberry Pi.

Installing and configuring Netatalk

Installing Netatalk has become really easy as most of the configuration is set up by default. At the time of writing this book, the version used was 2.3.3:

```
sudo apt-get install netatalk
```

Within 30 seconds, you will see your Raspberry Pi pop up in the shared section on your Macintosh. The default directory that is shared is the home directory of the user that you log in as, for example, user Pi.

Shares and Time Machine

We will create a few entries to use your external drive for the shares that you need, and this version of Netatalk also supports Time Machine.

You will need to edit this file to customize some of the settings as follows:

```
/etc/netatalk/AppleVolumes.default
#Ammend default to look like this
:DEFAULT: options:upriv,usedots,rw,tm
#Add this to end of the file
/nas/USB001/public "Public"
/nas/USB001/work "James Bond"
```

Read the configuration file for more options and adjusting security. After saving, you must restart Netatalk using the following command:

```
service netatalk restart
```

BitTorrent Sync

All the bad things that you may have heard about torrents were primarily caused by private companies who were deliberately placing infected files to try and track users sharing copyrighted material or malicious users who were after your personal details.

Sync is not a public network; it only uses the revolutionary peer-to-peer technology from conventional torrents, which allows you to share an unlimited amount of data with an unlimited number of computers. Files are not stored on the cloud. They are stored on all the computers that have BTSync installed on them, and you can control who has access and where these files will be stored. BTSync includes file versioning, sharing with mobile phones, LAN synchronizing, and delta updates. It also allows massive file transfers of gigabytes without any problem as long as your file system can support such large files.

Installing BTSync 2

At the time of writing this book, there were a few repositories that kept this package with startup scripts. A word of warning: do not trust sources other than the ones that are enabled by default. People can easily alter code and place their own version of the binary with some nasty backdoors. Go to the official website, or use the links provided by the official website.

We will create a new directory, download the ARM version of BTSync, and extract it as shown in the following command-line snippet:

```
mkdir ~/.btsync && cd ~/.btsync
wget http://download-cdn.getsyncapp.com/stable/linux-arm/BitTorrent-Sync_
arm.tar.gz -O btsync_arm.tar.gz
tar -xvf btsync_arm.tar.gz
```

We will create a service file. In /etc/init.d, create the btsync file and copy the following text:

```
#! /bin/sh
# /etc/init.d/btsync
#

# Carry out specific functions when asked to by the system
case "$1" in
start)
    /opt/btsync/bin/btsync --config /opt/btsync/bin/btsync.conf
    ;;
stop)
    killall btsync
    ;;
*)
    echo "Usage: /etc/init.d/btsync {start|stop}"
    exit 1
    ;;
esac

exit 0
```

We need to set correct permissions for the new file:

```
sudo chmod 755 /etc/init.d/btsync
sudo update-rc.d btsync defaults
sudo service btsync start
```

BTSync will now start every time your Raspberry Pi 2 reboots. You can check out the configuration file at /opt/btsync/bin/btsync.conf but the defaults work pretty well.

You can now navigate a browser on the same network to your Pi's address at http://raspberrypi:8888/gui.

In the GUI, add the directory on the hard drive. Now, install the application on your Mac OS X, Windows, Linux machine, or smart phone. Use the GUI to share directories between users. It can detect machines on the same network, which increases the speed of synchronization.

Sync tries its best to configure ports, and it uses protocols to communicate over the Internet. In theory, you can now call your friend on the phone, ask them to install Sync, and share the directory via an e-mail. They will now start seeing the same files as you.

> BitTorrent Sync 2 uses external servers for tracking purposes, but no actual files are stored on them; there is no public access to the tracker files.
>
> BitTorrent Sync claims to use SRP for mutual authentication and Perfect Forward Secrecy in which all data is then encrypted with AES-128 Counter Mode and unique session keys. It is a very complex way to ensure nobody can guess your key, not even BitTorrent. It is all dynamically generated on the fly, and then clients negotiate more keys during transfers. This sounds really good, but you will have to take them on their word as the project is closed source.

The hardware RAID

The Raspberry Pi does not have a SATA controller on board, and there is no way to attach extra hard drives except via USB ports. The cool thing is that you can get a USB RAID controller. This makes file storage on the Raspberry Pi a very attractive option. Technically, the peripheral needed here is called the USB SATA multiplier.

Configuration

There is no one-step guide to configuring these multipliers. Some need to be configured using software in Windows or Linux, while others may have DIP switches that configure the multiplier to a specific configuration.

Addonics is a well-known and fairly easy-to-source multiplier. You will need to search around on the Internet, online auctions, and shops for it. The prices are around the same as the Raspberry Pi but if you are looking for redundant storage, then these are the cheapest options you will find.

Massive storage

If you are looking to create really massive storage, you can easily daisy chain a multiplier with another, sometimes up to three or four times. Recently, Addonics developed another device that can be daisy chained infinitely!

Let's assume that we can daisy chain up to three levels, and we use 2 TB hard drives. We configure all the multipliers to span data across all drives with no redundancy; that is, five times five, times five. We end up with 125 usable SATA ports and a total of 250 terabytes of storage. This figure is highly impractical for home users because all these hard drives consume a lot of power. There are some people who have hard drive rigs such as these at home, so I would think using six multipliers to achieve 25 SATA ports would be a completely viable and cheap option for some readers! The following figure is a simple example of how to replicate one SATA port into five more ports using SATA port multipliers:

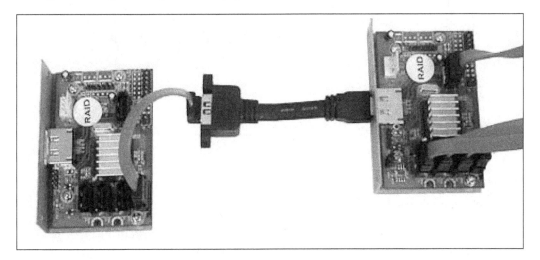

Redundant storage

We all have lost important data way too many times in our lives, so you should consider redundancy over massive storage. We can use a set of four 1 TB hard drives that are configured in RAID 5 + S. This gives us 3 TB of usable space. Also, if any one hard drive crashes, you can just replace it quickly and all the data that we resynchronize will be stored without any loss. The following is a figure explaining each feature of a SATA Port replicator:

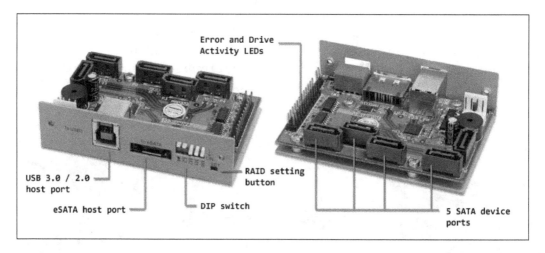

Summary

This chapter demonstrates that the Raspberry Pi is capable of doing anything that a normal computer or server can do. It is capable of sharing files with various platforms. You can connect to the Raspberry Pi using the latest secure FTP. It is capable of storing a great amount of data using some clever hardware add-ons.

In the next chapter, we will set up various gaming servers.

6
Setting Up Game Servers

As great as it would be to run a Counter Strike server on Raspberry Pi, it is just not possible due to the high requirements of running such game servers. Mostly, this is due to the shortfall of RAM, but some servers also require powerful processors to deliver low-latency performance for all players, which could be up to 24 players per game.

In this chapter, you will be introduced to open source games that have been developed by people with a passion for a particular genre of games. These games were reverse engineered, built from scratch, or just became popular due to their simplicity.

Updating to Jessie

At the time of writing this book, the main distribution for the Rasbperry Pi was still Debian Wheezy. Debian Jessie was added around June 2013 for testing on the Rasspbery Pi but is already used on desktop machines. As of April 2015, there seems to be a stable version for the Raspberry Pi. A lot of game server packages were updated only in Jessie because of newer dependencies.

You can upgrade the entire Raspberry Pi to Jessie, but you are advised not to do this until the official image is released. Instead, we will install selected, specific packages from Jessie while keeping the entire distribution stable in Wheezy. These steps can be skipped if you are already using Jessie.

Selective settings

We can add the following two lines to /etc/apt/sources.list:

```
deb http://mirrordirector.raspbian.org/raspbian/ jessie main contrib
non-free rpi
deb http://archive.raspbian.org/raspbian jessie main contrib non-free
rpi
```

The next step is to tell aptitude to use the `wheezy` repository for normal updates and that you would like to use Jessie from time to time. These settings should be typed into the file found at `/etc/apt/preferences`. Create this file if it does not exist:

```
Package: *
Pin: release n=wheezy
Pin-Priority: 900

Package: *
Pin: release n=jessie
Pin-Priority: 300

Package: *
Pin: release o=Raspbian
Pin-Priority: -10
```

After adding these settings and saving the files, run `sudo apt-get update`.

We will be using `apt-get` with an extra switch to use the new packages. You should only use this switch when it is advised. Upgrading core packages could result in unstable behavior. The syntax we will be using is as follows, where `<package>` will be replaced with the game package that we require in the following paragraphs:

```
sudo apt-get -t jessie install <package>
```

Game servers

We will only be focusing on running the server parts of games that do not require desktop interaction. Instead, you run the client on another computer and connect to Raspberry Pi. Some clients can run on Pi's X desktop, and they would do reasonably well on the Raspberry Pi 2 but might not be very pleasant.

OpenTTD

OpenTTD is a reimplementation of the original Transport Tycoon made by MicroProse. The game is dangerously addictive, and adding Internet play to the mix can give you an extra competitive edge.

You have to have a passion for logistics, strategy, and real-time simulation to enjoy this game. The goal is just something to do with controlling trains and trucks as efficiently as possible and make profit while transporting cargo.

Installing OpenTTD

The latest package is kept only on Jessie:

```
sudo apt-get -t jessie install openttd
```

Several libraries will be installed during this time. You may be presented with a blue screen, which asks you if you want to restart some services in order to complete the package installation. It is safe to agree to this. This can take several minutes to complete.

Configuring OpenTTD

The configuration file called `openttd.cfg` can be found at `~/.open`. It contains a few hundred settings that you can tweak according to your preferences, but some of the important ones are as follows:

- `lan_internet`: This sets the condition for the LAN access. For lan0, allow the Internet, and for lan1, use LAN only.

- `server_name`: This is a unique name to identify the server on the Internet.

- `server_advertise`: We set this to `true` so that it will be visible on the server list.

- `server_bind_ip`: We set this to `0.0.0.0`; this allows the address to bind to any network.

- `server_port`: For this, we keep the default value; this is how other people from the Internet will connect over to the network.

 To allow people to connect from the Internet, you should forward the 3979 and 3978 ports to the Raspberry Pi in your router.

Start the server with the following options:

```
./usr/games/openttd -D
```

Playing OpenTTD

You can now install and run OpenTTD on other computers and invite some friends to join you.

Click on **Multiplayer**, and select **Internet** if you have forwarded the ports for the game. Click on **find**, and a list of servers will be displayed.

Freeciv

> *"This is a free and open source empire-building strategy game inspired by the history of human civilization."*

> *– Freeciv*

The game reminds me of Civilization by Sid Meier. Its user interface is very similar, but once you start playing the game, you will notice a lot more features and possibilities that are built into the game.

Installing Freeciv

We can install the server from the Raspberry repository:

```
sudo apt-get -t jessie install freeciv-server
```

Several libraries will be installed during this time. You may be presented with a blue screen, which asks you if you want to restart some service in order to complete the package installation. It is safe to agree with this. This can take several minutes to complete.

Configuring Freeciv

The default settings are good enough for you to play straight away. You can start the server by typing the following in the console:

```
freeciv-server
```

> The server should not be run with the sudo command or as the root user but as a normal unprivileged user.

This will actually present you with another console provided by the `freeciv` server. You can adjust settings of the server by typing in commands. You can try to type in `help` and press **Enter**.

If you would like to publish your server to the online community, you need to forward port 5555 to the Raspberry Pi through your router, and then start the server with the extra command line called `--meta`.

Playing Freeciv

You can now install and run `freeciv` on your computer. If you are running the same versions of the server and client, you will see it in LAN.

OpenArena

OpenArena is a free, first-person shooter based on the Quake 3 engine. It aims to be a clone of Quake 3, but it replaces propriety content with brand new features.

Installing OpenArena

The server installation can take up to 500 MB. Make sure you have enough free space, and then we can install the game using the Jessie repository:

```
sudo apt-get -t jessie install openarena-server
```

Several libraries will be installed during this time. You might be presented with a blue screen, which asks you if you want to restart some services in order to complete the package installation. It is safe to agree with this. This can take several minutes to complete.

Configuring OpenArena

If you would like to share your server on the Internet, you should open and forward UDP ports 27960 and 27950 on your router. Go through the settings found at `/etc/openarena-server/server.cfg`:

- `set dedicated 2`: We use 2 for the Internet while 1 (default) is LAN
- `sv_hostname "Raspberry Pi"`: This is used to set the name of your server
- `sv_master1 "dpmaster.deathmask.net"`: This sets the Internet server that keeps lists
- `sv_maxclients 16`: This is the maximum amount or the number of clients that are allowed to connect
- `capturelimit 8`: This is used to set the capture limit in CTF
- `timelimit 15`: This is used to set the time limit
- `fraglimit 35`: This is used to set the frag limit
- `g_motd "This Pie is delicious!"`: This is used to set the message of the day
- `g_gametype 0`: This is used to set gametype to `Free for All`; it is also known as Deathmatch

You can find hundreds of extra settings on the OpenArena Wiki. Remember that the server must not be run as root.

The OpenArena server runs as a service. We should stop the service and run it on a console to make sure that everything runs fine. Once you are happy that everything is configured properly, you can start the service again:

```
sudo service openarena-server stop
/usr/games/openarena-server +exec /etc/openarena-server/server.cfg
```

Playing OpenArena

The game can be played on Windows, Mac OS X, or Linux. You should go to the website for platform-specific clients.

Minecraft

Minecraft is a sandbox indie game where you are in control of a person that can build anything you imagine. There are complex blocks that can be used or programmed to do various server-side calculations. If you would like to see the complete potential of Minecraft, you should visit BitVegas. This will be more difficult than the other servers as we need to install and configure a lot of dependencies.

Installing the Java Hard-Float

We will need to go to `https://jdk8.java.net/download.html`, accept the terms, and copy the link to the Linux ARM 32bit for this. Now, we need to download the file, ignoring any certificate problems:

```
sudo wget --no-check-certificate <URL>
```

Then, enter these lines into the console and replace `<filename>` with the latest file you that have downloaded:

```
mkdir -p /opt
sudo tar zxvf <filename> -C /opt
sudo /opt/jdk????/bin/java –version
```

 You can start typing the filename and then press **Tab**. This will autocomplete the filename or display a list of similar names for your convenience.

If you get a response from the version command line, then you now have Java Hard-Float installed on your Raspberry Pi.

Installing the Minecraft server

Minecraft servers are actively developed by various crowds, and there are many configurations to choose from. **Spigot** is a high performance Minecraft server implementation, and we can install it with the following command:

```
cd /home/pi
sudo wget http://ci.md-5.net/job/Spigot/lastStableBuild /artifact/Spigot-
Server/target/spigot.jar


# This is the command line use on Pi 2 1GB ram
sudo /opt/jdk1.8.0/bin/java -Xms512M -Xmx992M -jar /home/pi/spigot.jar
nogui


#This is the command line use on Model B with 512 ram
sudo /opt/jdk1.8.0/bin/java -Xms256M -Xmx496M -jar /home/pi/spigot.jar
nogui
```

It takes about 10 minutes to start up for the first time. Once it is ready, you can log on locally from another machine and explore your new world. You should exit shortly and configure the server for performance.

Configuring Minecraft

To allow players from the Internet to connect, you will need to open and forward the port called 25565 to the Raspberry Pi from your router.

These are the settings that seem to be best for running on the Raspberry Pi. You can adjust them as you go along:

```
server-name=Raspberry Picraft!
motd=Pie is Delicious
allow-flight=false
spawn-monsters=true
generate-structures=true
enable-query=false
enable-rcon=false
level-name=world
spawn-protection=16
online-mode=true
```

```
difficulty=1
gamemode=0
spawn-animals=true
Setting Up the Game Servers
view-distance=4
level-seed=
hardcore=false
snooper-enabled=false
level-type=DEFAULT
pvp=true
texture-pack=
max-players=20
server-ip=
max-build-height=240
spawn-npcs=true
server-port=25565
white-list=false
generator-settings=
allow-nether=false
```

Playing Minecraft

To connect to your server, you will need to put your Raspberry IP address in the network settings. If you would like other people to join from the Internet, you should read *Chapter 2, Preparing a Network*, to learn how to set up dynamic DNS.

Summary

In this chapter, you learned how to use another non-default Jessie repository and how to set up various gaming servers on the Raspberry Pi. You also learned how to install OpenTTD, Freeciv, and OpenArena from aptitude. We covered how to set up a high-performance Minecraft server using Java Hard-Float.

In the next chapter, we will be setting up live video streaming.

Streaming Live HD Video

7

In this chapter, we are going to use the official HD camera module designed by the Raspberry Pi Foundation. Thanks to the new quad core processor and the author of UV4L, we can now stream a video directly into a browser with low latency.

Before starting this chapter, you should have the camera module installed and enabled as described with the instructions included with the camera module. It is recommended to have 256 MB GPU RAM allocated.

This chapter is only suitable for the Raspberry Pi 2 or newer with the quad processor or better.

Installing UV4L

UV4L is a userspace webcam driver specifically designed for the Raspberry Pi. It also includes some other features that will be discussed in this chapter. U4VL is custom code that is written and developed by Luca Risolia, who runs the website `http://linux-projects.org`. We will add his repository to get the UV4L driver:

```
curl http://www.linux-projects.org/listing/uv4l_repo/lrkey.asc | sudo
apt-key add -
```

Add the following line to `/etc/apt/sources.list`:

```
deb http://www.linux-projects.org/listing/uv4l_repo/raspbian/ wheezy
main
```

 If you have not yet run `rpi-update`, then it is recommended to do it now. The `UV4L` driver requires the latest foundation kernels and modules to install properly.

Now we need to update the repository list, and then we can install the UV4L driver. We will do these with the following commands:

```
sudo apt-get update
sudo apt-get install uv4l uv4l-raspicam
sudo apt-get install uv4l-server uv4l-raspicam-extras
```

 The UV4L driver makes it really easy to stream video from the Raspberry Pi. Consider supporting Luca by visiting his website and donating to his cause or purchasing a serial key for the overlay module that is described later in the chapter.

Configuring the UV4L-RaspiCAM

The configuration file can be found at `/etc/uv4l/uv4l-raspicam.conf` and is used to configure the initial video stream. There are default settings that are used, and the following bullet points are settings found within the file that you may be interested in changing manually for your own use.

 These are some typical settings that you may want to use if capturing a stream using VLC. The driver is adaptive and will change configurations if you request MJPEG stream, or it will start a WebSockets stream from the browser, technically allowing you multiple streams. Multi-streaming is experimental, though.

Here are some typical settings:

- Encoding:

  Streaming: H264, mjpeg, jpeg, yuv420

  Specialist: nv21, yvu420, rgb565, rgb565x, rgb24, bgr24, rgba.

- Framerate:

  0 sets auto

  30 at 1080p

  60 at 720p

  90 at VGA.

- Bitrate: 17000000 (default value)

- The Intra-period: This is used for H264 only; if you experience artifacts in the stream, try adjusting this value. Usually, artifacts are caused by lost frames and poor network performance. The lower this value, the more bandwidth is used. A good start is FPS / 2.

- Quality:

  This applies to JPEG and MJEP streaming only

  85 is the default value.

- * text overlay: Uncomment the two properties as this will be required later in the chapter.

- * no preview: If you have a monitor connected to HDMI, you will see the original stream preview. Uncomment this if you are experiencing Raspberry Pi reboot with a 1 A power supply and Wi-Fi.

Most of these configuration settings can be altered through the web interface by navigating to `http://raspberrypi:8080`. The options with the * mark must be configured in the configuration file, and UV4L must be restarted.

Installing WebRTC

Web Real-Time Communication (WebRTC) is a protocol that allows modern web browsers to establish a peer-to-peer link to exchange data. UV4L uses WebRTC to create a socket to the Raspberry Pi and receive a live H264 video stream, eliminating the need for transcoding and allowing us to watch a high-quality, low-latency video directly in our browser.

To install the WebRTC module for `uv4l-server`, we just need to issue one command and restart UV4L:

```
sudo apt-get install uv4l-webrtc
sudo service uv4l_raspicam restart
```

WebRTC streaming

Please be aware that UV4L WebRTC streams in an adaptive bitrate and resolution. The bitrate and resolution streamed to the client will adaptively adjust based on the connection quality. This means that any configuration that you have applied will not apply to WebRTC streams, but the overlay will still work. It may also disconnect other streams that do not use WebRTC.

You can now navigate to `http://raspberrypi:8080`, and you will be presented with a screen similar to the following:

<u>UV4L</u> HTTP/WebRTC Streaming Server

- edit configuration file
- camera control panel
- audio/video stream via WebRTC
- video stream in MJPEG or JPEG (still captures)
- multi peer-to-peer audio/video conferencing
- stream audio/video to a Jitsi Meet Web Conference (what is Jitsi Meet?)

device: /dev/video0
current connections: 2, queued: 0, total handled: 2
max. simultaneous streams allowed: 3, max. threads: 5

---

contact donate!

You can click on `audio/video stream via WebRTC`. Then, on the next page, click on the **start** button. It may take a few seconds to establish a link, and if everything goes as planned, you will know see a live stream from the Raspberry Pi camera.

With the Raspberry Pi 1, it was extremely complicated to set up a stream similar to this one, leaving almost no resources left on the Pi at all. The WebRTC module is truly a time saver in terms of streaming from your Raspberry Pi.

Real time HTTP streaming

To configure the HTTP stream, you can click on the **Camera Control Panel** link on the UV4L web page and set the format and other options you would like.

Alternatively, if you don't want to access the webpage, you can just configure the `raspicam` configuration file as you need it, and then you can use the corresponding URL in VLC or a third-party app to capture the stream:

- HTTP/MJPEG: `http://raspberrypi:8080/stream/video.mjpeg`
- HTTP/Raw H264: `http://raspberrypi:8080/stream/video.h264`
- HTTP/JPEG: `http://raspberrypi:8080/stream/video.jpeg`

To receive a H264 stream using VLC, I have found that tweaking some of the plugin settings worked best for me:

1. Click on **Tools | Preferences**.

2. Click on **All** in the **Show settings** panel in the bottom-left corner.

3. Click on **Input / Codecs | Demuxers**.

4. Change the demux module from the **Automatic** to **H264** video demuxer.

5. Click on **Demuxers | H264**.

6. You will notice that it is set to 25 frames per second. Unfortunately, changing this value does not work as expected. You should rather change your configuration on the Raspberry Pi to stream at 25 frames per second.

7. On the Raspberry Pi, choose a suitable bit rate for your stream. On the LAN, this maybe the default, but on Wi-Fi, I suggest you try lower bitrates.

This configuration works best for higher quality streaming. It is necessary to change the VLC demuxer to H264 because it does not seem to be able to recognize the format on its own. You can also specify an additional option of :demux=h264, but I find that strictly setting the demuxer to H264 works better.

We also need to adjust the frame rate on the Raspberry Pi to 25 fps to match the default in the H264 module in VLC. Adjusting the frame rate in the module on VLC to 30fps did not help. The reason behind adjusting the frame rate is that I noticed strange artifacts on moving objects. This suggested bandwidth problems, but it even happened on the LAN.

I finally found this solution and realized that the Raspberry Pi was sending 30 fps while the demuxer was decoding at 25 fps, causing the key frames to be out of sync. As strange as this may sound, it really does produce a good quality stream, albeit with about 1+ seconds of buffering.

If you are experiencing no video, lots of artifacts, or long lags, refer to *Chapter 2, Preparing a Network* on how to run the iperf test to make sure you have good enough bandwidth. Bandwidth problems may also be caused by a poor power supply, especially if you are using a wireless adapter.

Web conferencing

In the latest version of UV4L, there is an interesting new feature for web conferencing with audio and video. This feature is built into the webrtc module, and no extra configuration is necessary.

Any WebRTC compatible device, such as a smart phone, note book, or standard desktop, with a modern browser can join into the conference by going to `http://raspberrypi:8080/conference`. This will work inside your LAN, but if you would like to allow connections from the Internet, you need to provide the correct IP address in the Signaling Server Field and open the necessary ports.

This works purely as a server and does not use the Pi's camera, but you can join the conference from your Raspberry Pi from within the X client and a browser. If you want to use audio on the Raspberry Pi, make sure you have `pulseaudio` installed and a compatible USB sound card with a microphone.

Streaming the X desktop

It is also possible to stream your actual X desktop using the UV4L driver. Consider it something like screen casting, similar to Miracast. If your smart TV's browser supports WebRTC, you can simply enter the URL and have a wireless video feed of the desktop on the TV.

To use this feature, we need to install an extra module.

```
sudo apt-get install uv4l-xscreen
```

You can then use `raspi-config` to `enable boot to desktop/scratch` to start up on the boot. As mentioned in the WebRTC section, the only caveat at the moment is that this will only work with a specific resolution. Other resolutions may be supported in the future. You will need to edit your `/boot/config.txt` file as follows:

```
framebuffer_width=640
framebuffer_height=480
framebuffer_depth=32
framebuffer_ignore_alpha=1
```

You can now log into your Raspberry Pi over SSH and issue the following command:

```
uv4l --driver xscreen --auto-video_nr --display :0 --framerate 10
--server-option '--port=9000'
```

Ignore all warnings. This command starts a new UV4L server and creates a device called `/dev/video1` that can be used with the same commands as described in the *real-time HTTP streaming* section. It creates the webserver under port 9000. Port 8080 still works and can continue to stream your webcam while streaming the X video separately.

You can view the video transmission at: `http://raspberrypi:9000/stream/webrtc`.

Text overlay

Text overlay is a feature that allows you to superimpose text lines onto video frames without any transcoding. The UV4L driver works extremely well with HD streams and framerates higher than 30, and supports mjpeg, H264, yuv420, and other video formats.

 When enabled, the image width and height should be a multiple of 16. For 1080p you would need to use 1920 x 1088, 720p would be 1280 x 720, and so on.

At the most basic level, text is read from a JSON-formatted file, which contains properties for each line's position, color, thickness, and scale. The default configuration file will display the video frame rate as it is being transmitted. The configuration file gets loaded when the camera is started for the first time, but it can be updated with a specific command, making heads-up displays (HUDs) a practical reality.

To enable the text overlay, you need to start the driver with the following /etc/uv4l/uv4l-raspicam.conf configuration before loading the camera page for the first time. You cannot enable this feature if there is already an ongoing stream:

```
text-overlay = yes
text-filename = /usr/share/uv4l/raspicam/text.json
```

The text.json file contains a sample of all the options that are available to you. It is a good idea to copy this file to /home/pi.

 If you plan on updating the file frequently, it is recommended to store the file in /tmp as the file will actually be stored in RAM.

After restarting the uv4l_raspicam service, you will now see some sample overlay text on your video stream.

You can edit the text.json file and execute the following command in the console for the overlay text to be updated:

v4l2-ctl --set-ctrl=text_overlay=1

This is a very basic approach to updating the overlay on your video stream, for example, running a separate program you wrote that will overwrite the file every so often and issue the refresh command.

Using this approach, you will not be able to update the overlay any faster than 1 second at a time. If you would like to achieve real-time overlay updates, refer to The HUD sample section.

More details about how to remove the `http://www.linux-projects.org` overlay are provided further on in this chapter.

Object detection and tracking

Object detection and tracking can be turned off and on at any time. This feature only works with the yuv420, H264, and mjpeg encodings.

This feature requires more CPU overhead depending on how complex a task you are doing. For example, on the Pi 2, you can use face recognition with 640 x 480 at 15 FPS with some heavy CPU usage. On the Pi 1, it is about half of this:

```
uv4l --driver raspicam --auto-video_nr --object-detection --min-
object-size 80 80 --main-classifier /usr/share/uv4l/raspicam/
lbpcascade_frontalface.xml --object-detection-mode accurate_detection
--width 320 --height 240 --framerate 15 --encoding h264
```

Removing the overlay watermark

I have been in contact with Luca Risolia, the author of UV4L, and he has agreed to provide you with an exclusive deal; as the reader of this book, you will be the very first person to know that he has agreed to provide you with a way to remove the white `http://www.linux-projects.org` watermark on the 3 Raspberry Pi's that you own!

All you need to do is send an e-mail to `info@linux-projects.com` with the following details from your Raspberry Pi by executing and copying the results of this command:

```
uv4l --driver raspicam --serial-number
```

I am sure Luca will be grateful for a small donation in return for three serial numbers, and this will allow him to continue to create more features for this excellent driver.

The HUD sample

As defined by Wikipedia, a heads-up display, also known as a HUD, is a transparent display that presents data without requiring users to look away from the main activity. The origin of the name comes from a pilot being able to view information with their head positioned up or straight ahead, instead of looking down at some instruments.

So, to stop us from looking down into the console, I thought it would be a nice idea to see some information about our Raspberry Pi directly on the video stream.

With some help from Luca, I have created the C++ code that allows you to update the overlay pretty much on every frame using the UV4L API directly, which means hardly any CPU overhead is used.

If you feel comfortable with C++11, I have provided the complete code sample on the code download page, and you can add your own variables.

I have also provided a compiled binary with a variety of popular resource variables that you can use easily place in the template file once, and will be updated in real time on your stream.

Using the overlay binary

The binary requires two parameters: the source video device and the source file, which will be referred to as the template file. The template file is exactly the same format as `text.json`, but the difference is that you construct the text fields with the inline variables listed here. It is recommended to copy your template file to `/tmp/file.tpl` and provide it as the source template.

You will also need to update the `uvl_raspicam.config` file to point to a new location, `/tmp/text.json` (not the template file), and restart the UV4L service. A new file will be created in `/tmp/text.json` from which the UV4L API call will read the replaced variables. Do not alter this file. Working with these files in `/tmp` is critical for achieving the best video performance but also eliminating I/O from your SD card, which may cause unnecessary wear during long periods of use.

 In case you are wondering, you can update the template `/tmp/file.tpl` file while the binary is running. The C++ binary file reads the template file using a stream open in read-only mode with minimal locks.

Use this command line to execute the binary:

```
./overlay /dev/video0 /tmp/text.tpl
```

Inline variables

Here are some useful variables from the general Raspberry Pi resources:

- `{sysnfo.cputemp}`

Wireless info (the default is `wlan0`):

- `{signfo.level}`: Signal strength
- `{signfo.quality}`: Signal quality
- `{signfo.bitrate}`: Bitrate

Network bandwidth (the default is `eth0`):

- `{nnfo.downspeed}`
- `{nnfo.upspeed}`

A sample text line will look like this:

```
"ETH0 UP: {nnfo.upspeed} CPU temp {sysnfo.cputemp}"
```

To change the default values you need to amend the C++ file and recompile it. If you are already going to edit the code, use the base code as an example and try to add something else. If you have never edited C++ or any other code, just try to understand the main class line by line, and by the time you get to the end, you will understand the basic C++.

Compiling the overlay code yourself

The C++ code was written in the C++11 standard, and it is necessary to install G++ version 4.8 to be able to compile this code. No extra libraries, such as `libboost`, are required for this sample:

```
sudo apt-get install g++-4.8
```

Once you have installed the latest G++, you can then simply compile the main code file and extra code files with any changes you have made by executing the following command:

```
sudo g++-4.8 -Ofast -std=c++11 *.cpp -o overlay
```

Luca has also provided a text-scrolling example that can be downloaded from `http://www.linux-projects.org/downloads/examples/uv4l-overlay.cpp`, but it requires the Boost C++ library. Unfortunately, the inclusion of this library causes the code to take considerably longer to compile. This is why I have removed all dependencies from the Boost library in my code; it provides a lot of extra support for tasks and structures used in modern programming languages and is worth a try:

```
sudo apt-get install libboost-all-dev
```

If you are a Visual Studio developer, you will be happy to know that I have created the overlay binary using Visual Studio with **VisualGDB**. VisualGDB allows you to write code with C++ intellisense in Visual Studio on your desktop. It will automagically copy your files and compile them on the Raspberry Pi over SSH. Another great feature is that you can debug the code running on the Pi within Visual Studio! You do not need to install any extra software on the Raspberry Pi. A tutorial on how to start using VisualGDB is available at `http://visualgdb.com/tutorials/raspberry/`.

There are other tutorials on the site you may find interesting. There is a 30-day trial you can use.

Summary

Streaming videos is still one of the most popular search terms on the Internet for the Raspberry Pi. There are a lot of different examples and solutions, some very complex some very easy.

Thanks to the work put into the UV4L driver, video streaming is becoming much easier to achieve. Compared to *Raspberry Pi Server Essentials*, *Packt Publishing*, my previous book, this chapter has been extremely shortened due to the easy that it has accomplishes now. Not only is it shorter, we have many more features to work with and can enjoy HD video streaming on the Raspberry Pi 2 with the smallest amount of effort.

In the next chapter, we will look at how to set up the Pi as a media center.

8

Setting Up the Pi as a Media Center Server

The Raspberry Pi has an HDMI output that is capable of streaming high definition audio video, and it also supports CEC to share remote control functions. In this chapter, we will look at how to use the Raspberry Pi as a media server directly from the command line, displaying images and playing audio. We will briefly look at some other solutions that people have come up with, and finally install OSMC (previously known as RaspBMC—an XBMC media center), which uses hardware decoding and CEC out of the box.

If you are going to use Raspbian for these examples, it would be advisable to allocate some more GPU RAM. A recommended value is 512MB for the Raspberry Pi 2. You can change core system settings by typing `raspi-config` in the command line.

Slideshows

Linux users are familiar with the command-line program called `fbi` (frame buffer image viewer). We will connect a widescreen monitor or HD TV using an HDMI cable.

 You should be aware that square aspect computer monitors smaller than 19 inches or non-HD TVs are generally not supported with HDMI output.

There is a project called **HDMIPi** that offers an affordable 9-inch, HD 1280 x 800 LCD screen, which plugs into the HDMI port without any extra parts. There are other smaller LCD screens available, but they can be quite expensive, and you need to check compatibility.

Using fbi

On the Raspberry Pi, you can load original sized photos from high quality cameras, but it is recommended to use a fast class 10 SD card or other fast storage. The new quad core processor speeds up loading times considerably. On the Raspberry Pi 1, it was recommended to downsize photos to help loading times. With the Raspberry Pi, it is still advised to downsize, but you can easily keep the images in an HD resolution, which is near 3 megapixels (2048 x 1536). To produce the crispest images, it suggested to match the image resolution to the display resolution and the aspect ratio.

Use the following command lines over SSH. This will install fbi and start a simple slideshow over SSH, but the output will be the attached monitor on HDMI:

```
sudo apt-get install fbi
cd /home/pi/photos
sudo fbi -T 1 -a -noverbose -t 5 *.*
```

fbi will now loop through all the images in the directory, changing them every 5 seconds until you stop it.

The T -1 command tells fbi to use the terminal one output (in SSH only), which will be the HDMI port. We tell it to auto resize the images to fit the screen, while -a -t 5 changes the image every 5 seconds, and -noverbose disables any debugging information.

You will notice that fbi does not block the console and runs in the background. It is possible to run fbi again, and it will not complain about another instance. However, this may cause out-of-memory errors and unwanted behavior.

To stop fbi, we use the killall command:

```
sudo killall fbi
```

Playing videos

We can play video and audio files using OMXPlayer, which was specifically designed by the XBMC project, and it uses hardware decoding on the Raspberry Pi. Since OMXPlayer uses hardware decoders, it is possible for you to use any additionally purchased video licenses.

OMXPlayer requires at least 256 MB GPU RAM to run.

OMXPlayer for video playback

Download an MP4 file onto the Raspberry Pi (for example, we can use the site `http://www.hd-trailers.net/` to find some links) and we will use OMXPlayer to play video and sound to the HDMI port. You can also use RTMP streams directly instead of video files. Replace the URL in `wget` with an existing file on the Internet:

```
sudo apt-get install omxplayer
cd /tmp
sudo wget http://videosite.com/filename.mp4
omxplayer -o hdmi filename.mp4
```

Playing audio

The latest Raspbian image comes with all the sound drivers and utilities installed. The packages that are used belong to ALSA. The Raspberry Pi has no way to record audio as it has no microphone jack, and the GPIO pins are all digital. To record audio using GPIO, we need to use an A/D (analog-to-digital) device or a USB sound device that has a microphone input.

Aplay for audio playback

The following is a pre-installed package that plays WAV files:

```
cd /tmp
wget http://goo.gl/Ps3paV
mv Ps3paV siren.wav
aplay siren.wav
```

OMXPlayer for audio playback

OMXPlayer is not just used to play videos. It also supports the playback of audio files, such as MP3 files, and it will try to use hardware decoding if possible:

```
omxplayer audio-test.mp3
```

Using AirPlayer

There is a project called **shairport** that works really well on the Raspberry Pi. It does not support videos or photos, but streaming music in it is very stable. We will need to get the project and compile it. This will only take a few minutes:

```
cd /tmp
git clone -b 1.0-dev git://github.com/abrasive/shairport.git
cd shairport
sudo ./configure && sudo make && sudo make install
```

The files on /tmp will be deleted during the next boot, which is fine because the binaries are now installed on the Raspberry Pi. Run the server with the following command and the AirPlay icon will show up on your Apple devices that play music:

```
shairport -a 'ShairPortPi'
```

This will block the console, and you will see some messages pop up from time to time about packets, but this is normal.

Using alsamixer

You can log into another SSH console and control the volume using **alsamixer**. The Raspberry Pi only has one output by default, and pressing the up or down key will make it louder or quieter:

```
alsamixer
```

Installing OSMC

OSMC is a free and open source media center, which was originally known as RaspBMC; it is based on XBMC. In this section, we will burn a new image on the SD card. You can either use another SD card or wipe the one you have been using until now.

We can use a UI installer made for Windows, Mac OS X, and Linux:

1. Open your browser and navigate to https://osmc.tv/download.
2. Select the UI download link, which matches the operating system that you will burn the network from; download it and run it.
3. Select your language and then select Raspberry Pi 2.

4. On the following screen, try and select the latest version.

 Network image means that on the first boot, it will download the latest files, so it recommended to connect a wired network with Internet access for first boot.

The UI installer also gives us an option to install OSMC on a USB drive instead of an SD card. If you select this option, you will need a USB storage device connected during the first boot. You will also need a keyboard.

The first boot can take about 10 minutes to complete, after which it will reboot and the installation will be complete.

Configuring OSMC

OSMC can be configured from the user interface, but you can still log into SSH to install your own services or tweak some advanced settings. The default root login and password is OSMC, and you also get a web remote if you navigate your browser to http://osmc.local.

 On the remote page, you can use your keyboard arrows to control the user interface instead of clicking on the buttons.

Enabling other codecs

OSMC uses OMXPlayer, which was maintained by XBMC. As we know, OMXPlayer uses the Pi's hardware to decode videos and render the GUI.

If you have MPEG-2 or VC-1 encoded files, you can simply purchase licenses and enter codes using the OSMC interface. The H264 codec is already licensed in the price of the Raspberry Pi. Do this by navigating to: **Programs** | **OSMC Settings** | **Pi Config** (Raspberry ICON) | **GPU Mem & Config** and then enter your keys and reboot the system.

Wireless configuration

You should have been able to setup wireless connection during the first setup wizard if you had a wireless adapter plugged in. You can still configure Wi-Fi, and if your adapter supports it, you can also enable tethering (known as an Access Point), which is a great feature to extend your Wi-Fi range if your Raspberry Pi is connected via Ethernet. Navigate to **Programs** | **OSMC Settings** | **Network** (3 CONNECTED CIRCLES ICON)

Media sources

You can start to add the locations of the files that are stored on the USB drive. To do so, navigate to the following options:

- **Videos | Files | Add Videos**
- **Music | Add Music**

If you have a hard drive or USB stick inserted, you will be able to browse into the location. To access Samba or NFS, you need to type in a specific prefix before the IP address of your NAS to specify the required protocol:

- `smb://192.168.0.1/movies`
- `nfs://192.168.0.1/music`

Using add-ons

OSMC has a single repository for add-ons, but you can also install custom add-ons. You can find some great add-ons in the following repository:

Programs | Get More...

A lot of add-ons are getting ported to OSMC, and over time, you should find more and more interesting programs to install and use.

On the Raspberry Pi, you can also access a limited set of OSMC App Store programs:

Programs | OSMC Settings | App Store (Shopping Cart Icon)

AirPlay

As an Apple user, you will appreciate that OSMC can be used as a target to stream your media into:

Settings | Services | AirPlay | Allow Airplay Content

You will now find the AirPlay icon on your Apple devices.

Enabling CEC and remotes

CEC (**Consumer Electronics Control**) is a standardized protocol used in new
televisions, media players, and sound equipment. You need to have everything
connected using HDMI cables. In general, most remote controllers or systems allow
these functions. CEC is enabled by default, but you can change the settings as you
like. To do this, navigate to **Settings** | **System** | **Input Devices** | **Peripherals** | **CEC**.

If you have a smart TV using a CEC compliant HDMI cable, you should be able
to control the volume and navigate OSMC using the arrow buttons. More support
varies between devices.

You can also look at enabling other remotes in the system configuration. You may
need to manually configure Bluetooth or IR adapters to get these enabled. Navigate
to **Programs** | **OSMC Settings** | **Remotes** (Remote Icon).

Performance optimization

OSMC will run best on the Raspberry Pi 2, and you do not need to change
any settings.

There is a Raspberry Pi installer too, which is already tweaked for best performance
and lacks a lot of the fancy stuff, but it will play HD video.

Overclocking

Generally, it is not recommended to overclock the Raspberry Pi because it tends to
create problems with networking and stability. But if you have a good reason to
do so, then the option can be found here: **Programs** | **OSMC Settings** | **Overclock**
(Gauge Icon). You can select **Turbo**, a predefined overclock setting, or set your own
custom range.

Summary

In this chapter, you learned how to play audio, make slideshows, and watch videos
from the console. We also explored how to install a new operating system based on
RaspBMC, which is known as OSMC.

In the next chapter, we will look at how to run your Raspberry Pi using batteries.

9
Running Your Pi from a Battery's Power Source

You would typically run your server from a mains powered USB adapter. The Raspberry Pi is very small, and unlike full desktop PCs, it can run from batteries for an extended period of time if the battery setup has been done properly.

You may find the need to run the Raspberry Pi using batteries for remote controlled applications, for example, weather stations in remote areas, a remote controlled car, and similar situations.

The most common problems with embedded device are related to power. You purchased a 2 A power supply, but one thing you cannot see is how much noise the power supply generates.

This chapter will be short, but I will demonstrate how to create a long lasting, super clean, 99.8% noise-free power source. This is great for wireless communications that rely on clean and stable power sources.

Hardware requirements

If you are really serious about running your Raspberry Pi from batteries, you will have to prepare a budget for some extra equipment. These requirements will not clear out your bank account, but I will also include more expensive solutions and their benefits. This chapter is based on the minimum required equipment, which I typically use.

The minimum requirements are as follows:

- A battery charging station
- NiMH battery packs
- A voltage regulator

These are the minimum parts required to get a fairly decent and safe battery power source.

The battery charging station and voltage regulator can be reused for years to come, and the only further expense will be new batteries or higher quality equipment parts.

The remaining chapter will use these parts as my test rig, and the estimated price of each component is as follows:

- Charger: IMAX B6 (35 EUR/40 USD)
- Batteries: 2 x 1500 mAh 6.0V NiMH High power series (18 EUR/22 USD)
- Voltage regulator: 3 A/5 A UBEC with capacitor (4 EUR/6 USD)

Charging stations

This will be the most expensive part that you will need to acquire, but it is only a one-off expense. The charging station that I recommend is the well-known IMAX B6. It can charge a variety of batteries: Li-ion, LiPo, LiFe, NiCd, NiMH, as well as Pb. It has built-in safety features; it is very reliable and compact, pretty much the cheapest all-round charging solution to be found.

One last advantage to this charger is that you can power it using any kind of power pack between 12V and 18V. A caveat is, though, the closer to 12V you go, the higher the amps you need on the power brick, but it also depends on the rate at which you are charging your batteries. If you decide to get fast charging batteries, use a higher voltage and amp power pack. Take a look at next image:

 I strongly advise that you try source a genuine product if you would like to guarantee the longest life of your batteries. Using imitation products maybe safe enough, but try and reduce your top-charging limits or follow calibration instructions to prevent over-charging. Always charge batteries in a safe and well ventilated room away from flammable objects and out of reach of children.

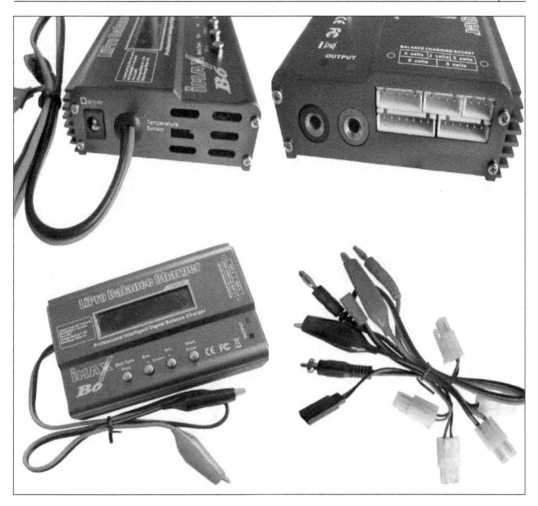

Battery packs

In my shortlist, I recommended NiMH (nickel-metal hydride) batteries because they are the safest batteries to use. These batteries do not become volatile when overcharged; in other words, you don't have to worry about the violent explosions that may happen with other types of battery. Overcharging these batteries will cause permanent damage, and the batteries must be replaced if that ever happens.

They have a fast self-discharge rate though, so they will not last long if fully charged and stored for later use. They are best used shortly after charging them.

An important factor is that they are pretty cheap to purchase. With the recent nano cell NiMH technology, you can pay slightly more to benefit from even better power output and capacities than leading Li-Po batteries. Look at the following image:

Voltage regulator

You maybe wondering why we don't just use 5V batteries to power the Raspberry Pi and reduce the cost of extra batteries and voltage regulators.

It all depends on the same principle as electricity in your home. The power station transports power in extremely high voltages exceeding tens of thousands of volts, but your computer only requires 12V to run.

The answer to all of this is Ohm's law. To understand this law in the simplest terms, you can imagine a seesaw with volts on one side and amps (the current) on the other side. Look at the following image:

The more volts you have, the fewer amps you need to use. The more amps you have, the fewer volts you need to provide. Ohm's law is universal and easy to adjust, but you still have to remember about resistance, which always works against you on each side of the seesaw, and this is related to the thickness of the wire you are using.

Using a 2 x 6V (12V) battery pack power supply to power a 5V system, we get a few benefits:

- We can provide higher constant power (amps) for a consistent period of time
- We can use the battery cells down to the very last volt; it will give us without losing power to the Raspberry Pi
- It is much easier to provide peak power (bursts of high power demand), which is great if you want to use motors or transmit high power bursts of data, and it is more efficient to do so with higher voltages
- Generally, this is the most stable configuration in this scenario for the Raspberry Pi

Ohm's Law

The following diagram is a simplified version of Ohm's law. It demonstrates all the calculations you need to work out a specific value, as discussed earlier. As a simple example, if you want to work out how many Amperes you need, you find the Amperes heading and pick a suitable equation. A suitable equation is one where you can fill in all the unknowns on the right-hand side. Apply the calculation and there is your answer:

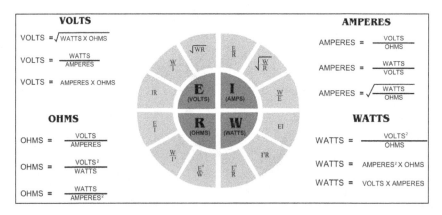

Discharge curves

When a battery cell starts to deplete, the voltage it provides drops a lot faster in the last 10% of its capacity. Looking at this graph, you can easily understand what this curve looks like at various discharge rates. If we used a 5V battery source, the Raspberry Pi would only run for about 60% of the batteries, power as it will soon drop below the 4.9V required for stable operation. But if we use higher voltage cells, we can utilize every last drop of voltage to keep the Raspberry Pi going:

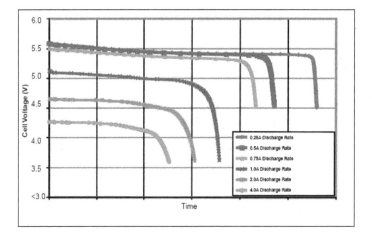

Discharge characteristics

As the voltages drop in each cell, the voltage regulator draws more power (amps) from the batteries to keep the output voltage stable. Remember the seesaw effect and Ohm's law? The last bit of power gets used up very quickly but constantly provides stable output power for the Pi:

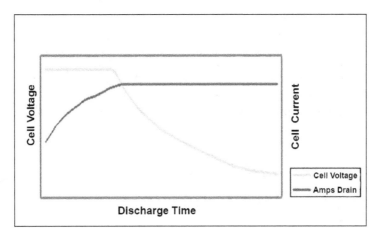

Putting it all together

To find all the extra parts, such as connectors and wires, you should visit your nearest RC hobby shop. You can buy all the parts and crimp everything yourself, but there are also premade wires for this exact setup.

I strongly recommend that you power your Raspberry Pi 2 via the USB connector. The Raspberry Pi Foundation has taken extra care to create a new power filtering system on the Raspberry Pi 2 to help stabilize the Raspberry Pi. Mostly because of all the strange USB power supplies out there, extra filtering and protection is always good.

If you have any extra peripherals, it would be best to connect them directly to the voltage regulator output instead of powering it from the Pi's GPIO or USB port. This will take unnecessary stress away from the Raspberry Pi, and the voltage regulator will easily handle higher loads.

How long will it last?

Battery capacities are measured using mAh (milli Ampere hour):

- By adding batteries in series, such as in this design, you do not gain more capacity but more voltage

- By adding batteries in parallel, you gain more capacity but stay at the same voltage.
- Finding the best balance depends on your requirements

To properly calculate how long your batteries will run can become a very complex calculation. You need to take a lot of things into consideration. In this design, using a higher voltage gives us more time because the voltage regulator needs to use less current (amps); a higher draw of charge reduces battery usability.

In an ideal world, you could say that we will be able to supply 1,500 milliamps per hour. This is 1.5 amps for an entire hour. If you want to extend battery life, you can add a separate battery circuit, such as the one demonstrated in this chapter, in parallel to the existing one. So, this would give you 1.5 amps for 2 hours or 3 amps for an hour.

In my own experience, I was able to stream an HD video over Wi-Fi to another computer on my network for nearly 3 hours.

Summary

You learned that running on batteries can quickly become a complicated task if you do not understand Ohm's law and some fundamental characteristics of batteries.

Using this tested design, you should be able to scale your requirements a lot more easily now, but I encourage you to always do more research when changing certain aspects of this design.

If in doubt, find a well-recommended RC hobby shop; the principles they use in this type of equipment is exactly the same here, and you will have all the parts and knowledge right there.

In the next chapter, you will learn how to install Windows IoT and create a simple Universal Application in Visual Studio Community.

10
Windows IoT Core

Windows IoT Core's main target is education and hobbyist users. It does have a GUI stack but is limited to Microsoft's **Universal App Platform (UAP)**, which is not a bad thing if you are interested in developing C# applications using XAML or HTML.

You are not strictly limited to the previously mentioned technologies. Microsoft tries to support a few other programming languages, such as C++ and Python with UAP SDK, but also native Win32 applications or services with some limitations.

The other benefit of developing universal apps is that you can install them on any device running Windows 10, even a full desktop. So, it is easy to distribute one code base to the Raspberry Pi 2, Intel Galileo, or MinnowBoard for embedded applications. Also, for remote managing console to your Windows 10 Phone, Tablet, Desktop, or Xbox.

Windows IoT comes with a lot of criticism from the Linux community as to why Microsoft even bothered doing all of this. Essentially, the point is not to replace Linux or try to displace Linux users but help more people to get involved with embedded prototyping. As a .NET developer, you will appreciate that you can finally create apps within a smooth workflow for embedded devices using the IDE that you love. Visual Studio, with full debugging capabilities with the ability to embed your favorite NuGet packages on a device that will measure the temperature of your aquarium.

 As of writing this chapter, appreciate that IoT has only been released; there are many issues that are still to be resolved and many more features to be added, so it will only get better from here on.

Getting started

To fully benefit from this chapter, you will need a Windows 7 or better desktop machine. Windows 10 is recommended but not essential.

To create universal applications for Windows, IoT will need to install Visual Studio 2015. You can install a completely free version called Community edition. Only 2015 supports universal apps. You can also create other types of projects in the Community edition completely free.

To get started with developing universal apps, you must have Visual Studio 2015. You can download the Community edition for free, but you need to create a live account and log into the account in the Visual Studio community to keep your free subscription active.

Flashing IoT

It is recommended to use Windows 10 desktop to download and burn the IoT image to an SD card. To get your image, you need to open https://dev.windows.com/en-us/iot and click on **Get started now**. You can then click on the **Rasperry Pi 2** and follow the steps there.

The SD card image is distributed in an FFU format supported only on Windows 10. To be able to burn it on an older version of Windows, we need to convert the image into a raw image file.

Python for Linux or Windows 7 and 8

Windows 10 has a new version of the DISM binary, which is used to burn the FFU image file types onto SD cards. In previous version of Windows, we will need to use Python. Python is also used on Linux-based machines.

If you have python installed on your Windows or Linux machine, you can use a script created by somebody that goes by the nick name of t0x0, and it can be downloaded from the following location. This script works both on Python for Windows and Python for Linux: https://raw.githubusercontent.com/t0x0/random/master/ffu2img.py

At this point, you will need to install Python 2.7 or a newer version for Windows, and you can get the latest installation files from https://www.python.org/downloads.

Copy the FFU2IMG Python script into the directory where you extracted the Windows IoT image. Open a command window, navigate to the directory, and use the following command to convert the image:

```
python ffu2img.py Flash.ffu
```

Then, you can flash the image onto an 8 GB minimum SD card from your Linux machine:

```
sudo dd bs=1m if=Flash.img of=/dev/<you_SD_card>
```

Or you can use Win32 DiskImager to burn the image from Windows, as described in *Chapter 1, Getting Started with the Raspberry Pi* for Rasbpian.

The first boot

Insert your SD card, plug in a wired internet connection and an HDMI display, and turn on the power. The first boot will take a few minutes with some screen flashing and strange looking graphics or text. It will automatically reboot, and you will see a screen with a language selection. If you don't have a keyboard hooked up, the default (English) will get connected automatically; and then, you will see a screen similar to this one:

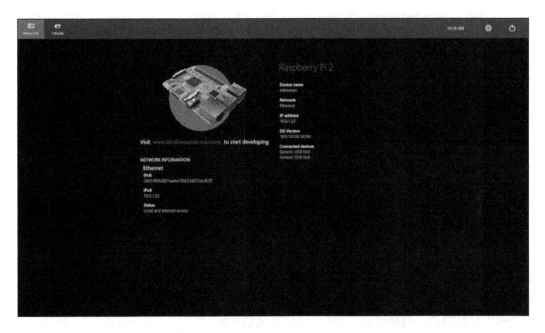

On this screen, you will see the IP address assigned to the Raspberry Pi. You can type the IP with the port 8080 address into your browser, and you will be presented with a web GUI.

The default username is administrator and the password is p@ssw0rd.

Remote connections

You can connect to Windows IoT by either using PowerShell in Windows or SSH connections, which will present you with a PowerShell command line running on Windows IoT.

The easiest way is to connect using SSH with Putty or similar as you would normally connect to any Linux-based machine.

To connect from Windows using PowerShell, perform the following:

1. Click on the **Start** menu and start typing `powershell`.
2. Right-click on **Powershell** and click on **Run As Administrator**.
3. Then, we need to type in a few commands in order to connect to IoT for the first time:

   ```
   net start WinRM
   Set-Item WSMan:\localhost\Client\TrustedHosts -Value <IP Address>
   ```

After this, you will be able to connect from Windows PowerShell to IoT PowerShell using the following command:

```
Enter-PSSession -ComputerName <IP> -Credential localhost\Administrator
```

> The connection process may take up to 30 seconds.
>
> When a connection is established, you will see the IP Address of your device before the prompt.

Visual Studio (VS)

In this section, we will go through how to prepare Visual Studio 2015 for IoT, and we will also take a look at the Hello World application to get familiar with the IDE.

Installing Visual Studio 2015

Use your favorite browser to search for **Visual Studio 2015 Community edition,** which is completely free to use without any time limits; download and install it.

After installing VS start it up once and log in, if required, to the Live account you used to download VS. Once it all seems loaded up we will need to shut it down to install the IoT templates required to develop for the Raspberry Pi (or other embedded devices running Win 10 IoT)

Once again, use your favorite search engine and search for **Windows IoT Core Project Templates**. You should use the official Microsoft `visualstudiogallery`. `msdn` link. There may be important messages there, so read those. Click on the **Download** button and run the executable. This will install additional **Universal Windows Platform** (**UWP**) templates that will not only enable you to write background applications on unheaded Pis for Visual Studio but also specific libraries that we will be using in universal apps.

Start Visual Studio up again, and find the new template under C#. Verify that the template has installed correctly:

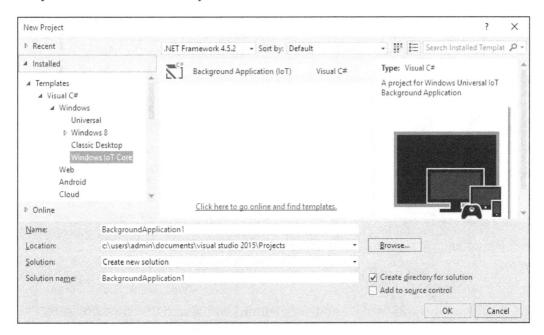

The Hello World application

This application will require you to have a monitor connected as we are first going to create a Windows Universal Application. It also shows you how to prepare your solution so that it can be used on the Raspberry Pi:

1. We will create a new project using this template; navigate to **Templates | Visual C# | Windows | Universal | Blank App** (Universal).

2. Give it the name of `HelloWorld` and click on **OK**.

3. You may be prompted to **Enable Developer Mode** if you are using Windows 10; navigate to **Settings | Update And Security | For Developers**.

4. The final step will be to add a reference to the IoT extensions required for the Raspberry Pi specific features, such as GPIO.

5. Right-click on **References** | **Add Reference** | **Universal Windows** | **Extensions** and check **Windows IoT Extensions for the UWP**.

Windows is designed using the XAML mark up. If you have ever worked with Silverlight, then you should be familiar with XAML. XAML is a general purpose object instantiation language, which is mostly declarative, such as HTML, but with an XML twist. But no need to worry about the low-level mark up as Visual Studio allows you to design visually!

 There is also a dedicated software called Blend that is purely used to create complex XAML layouts for applications that may require them.

1. In the **Solution Explorer** snap in Windows, locate and double-click on **MainPage.xaml**.

2. A new, blank designer view will open.

3. Select 40" IoT Device from the top because we will be making this view for an IoT device with a large screen. There are options for smaller screens too if you are using a mini LCD perhaps. This helps you lay out your design within a perspective view. In advanced techniques, you can create separate views for various devices using separate XAML files. These will all scale as best as possible to the available screen.

4. You can now expand the **Toolbox** on the right-hand side and have a look under **XAML Controls**.

5. From the Toolbox, click and drag button control onto the white designer area. Then, drop it in **TextBlock**.

6. Resize the button control to be larger, as it may have dropped in at a really small size.

7. While the button control is selected, change your **Snap** in view (in the right) to **Properties**.

8. Find the **Common** tab and change the content value to change the text that is displayed on the button; for example, Hello Word!

9. You can also change some properties for the text block, for example, the font size.

10. Then double-click on the button in the design view. This creates a code snippet; change the view to the code area, and position your cursor on the button click event code:

In the code, we will change the textBlock.Text value using this one line of code:

```
this.textBlock.Text = "Hello World!";
```

Deploying the application

It is very simple to deploy the application to the Raspberry Pi, but first, we will change the package name. Doing this is not that obvious unfortunately, but follow these steps:

1. In the **Solution Explorer Snap** window, click on the **Solution Explorer Snap** in tab.

2. Right-click on the **HelloWorld** project (not the Solution) and **Properties**.

3. Navigate to Package **Manifest** | **Packaging**.

4. The default value in the Package name is a Unique ID, and this is the name of the process that will be created on IoT. For now, we can change this to **HelloWorld** without spaces. When you want to publish an app to the store, you will need to use **NameSpace**, for example, My.RaspberryPi.HelloWorld.

5. Press *Ctrl + S* to save the solution, then close the window.

Now, to publish, we need to change a few settings and select the target device:

1. Change the x86 value in the top toolbar to ARM.

2. Next, to the green Play button, there is a small drop-down button; click on it and select the **Remote machine**.

3. This will bring up a new window, which automatically discovers Windows IoT devices running on your network. Make sure your Raspberry Pi is booted into the Windows 10 Dashboard app.

4. Click on the device entry found under **Auto Detected** and then **Select** (you will only need to do this once per session).

5. The project will build; if there are no errors, it will get published on the Raspberry Pi and run your application. Visual Studio is not in Debug Mode!

6. On the Raspberry Pi, click on your button, and the text box will be updated with the text you entered in the code earlier.

7. To stop debugging, click on the red **Stop** button.

You have now created your first Universal Application for the Raspberry Pi.

Debugging

One of the greatest features in Visual Studio is the debugging functionality. All these features are already enabled on Windows 10 IoT installed on your Raspberry Pi, and no extra configuration is required.

After you click on **Deploy** (the green start button), Visual Studio automatically goes into debug mode. In this mode, you cannot change any of the code; you can add or remove breakpoints, view output in the debug console, and use various other debug tools.

Visual Studio will also automatically break on unexpected errors and take you to the code that caused this exception with details about the problem.

As a long-time C# developer, I can admit that these errors might not make a lot of sense sometimes. The best thing is to search the Web for part of the error message and see what other developers have done to correct the problem. Stack Overflow usually provides high-quality answers for many ambiguous error messages.

Breakpoints

While the application is in the code edit mode, look at the source code of the button that we created earlier. You can add or remove breakpoints by clicking on the dark grey bar at the left, which will highlight the line of code in red:

```
        {
            public MainPage()
            {
                this.InitializeComponent();
            }

            private void button_Click(object sender, RoutedEventArgs e)
            {
                this.textBlock.Text = "Hello World!";
            }
        }
    }
```

Click on **Deploy and run**. Your break point will be hit before when you click on the button. To continue, click on the green Play button again, or *F10* for step over, or *F11* to step in (if it is a method you created or the source code is available)

Unhandled exceptions

To experience this feature, we will create a deliberate unhandled exception. It would be nice to demonstrate a Stack Overflow, but let's stick with a basic arithmetic function:

1. Under your break point, add these lines of code, and do not add any breakpoint to them:

```
int zero = 0;
this.textBlock.Text = (0 / zero).ToString();
```

2. Click on **Deploy and run**.

3. Click on the button on the IoT device and your first break point will become a hit.

4. Press **Continue** to continue executing the code.

5. Straight after continuing that you should get an unhandled exception message:

```
DivideByZeroException was unhandled by user code
```

This is a simple, self-explanatory exception. If you ever run into deeper water, you can use **View Detail…** under action to reveal some more debugging information.

These types of exception cause the application to crash whether you are in the Debug or Release mode.

If you suspect that an operation may result in an unhandled exception, for example, lots of arithmetic calculations, working with indexes, long running operations, or external calls, you can wrap this code in try block, which will prevent your application from crashing.

Amend the divide by the zero code as follows:

```
try
{
int zero = 0;
this.textBlock.Text = (0 / zero).ToString();
}
catch (Exception ex)
{
this.textBlock.Text = ex.ToString();
}
```

You can use the method to display error messages to the user or log exceptions to a database.

Samples

There is a large sample code package available to download from the code area. These are official Microsoft Samples, and they demonstrate not only how to create more advanced applications but also how to use the GPIO and other features on the Raspberry Pi.

Windows 10 IoT WebGUI

You can access your Raspberry Pi via your browser. Simply enter the IP with port 8080 and use the default username and password provided earlier in this chapter.

As time goes on, this page will be updated to support more features and may even completely change in the future. For now, we have access to various common commands, such as `Shutdown`, `reboot`, `processes`, `live performance graph`, and so on.

Setting up the startup app

The following are the steps to set up the startup app:

1. You can click on **Apps** on the left-hand side menu.
2. From the installed apps, find your app and click on it.
3. Once it is selected, click on **Set Default**.
4. You application will now start up after each boot:

5. Click on **Reboot** to test it.

WebGUI will still be available while your application runs.

Peripherals

I tried to plug in various devices and see what happens with most of them not doing anything. Popular ones seem to work, such as a USB mouse and keyboard transceiver.

Just remember that power is still an issue on USB, so it may be a good idea to use a powered hub.

You can find more information on supported devices by visiting: `http://ms-iot.github.io/content/en-US/win10/SupportedInterfaces.htm`.

Bluetooth

Bluetooth is still a fairly new addition to Windows IoT as of writing this chapter. I tried a generic Bluetooth dongle (unbranded), and it was installed successfully. It found my TV and my Bluetooth keyboard while I was on WebGUI.

I was successful in pairing my keyboard and navigating the screen.

You may also succeed in paring Bluetooth serial port transceivers as it seems to be supported on generic Bluetooth.

Wireless

Wireless support has been rapidly extended since the release candidate, and it supports the official Raspberry Pi dongle and other popular chipsets used in many other brands.

Summary

Even though Windows has various other ARM and MCU systems, Windows IoT was developed from a blank canvas. With time, the support will continue to grow for new devices and other ways to develop applications.

If you are interested in learning C# or are already a seasoned C# developer, this finally looks like the light at the end of the tunnel for an alternative embedded OS, other than the ever dominating *nix operating systems that were designed for these sorts of devices years ago.

There are many advantages in using Visual Studio and the Universal App architecture, but as of writing this chapter, there is still a lot of work to do for Microsoft.

11
Running Your ownCloud

This chapter covers how to install the open source ownCloud on to the Raspberry Pi 2, which is a great, free, self-hosted alternative to services such as DropBox, Google Drive, or Live Drive.

If you feel like you would like full control over the data, how you share it, and who can access it, ownCloud is a great solution. It is a self-hosted file sync and share server, which provides access through a web interface, the sync clients of WebDAV.

There are clients available for most operating systems, but even when you don't have a client, you can always use a modern browser to get straight into your data.

Installation

As of this writing this chapter, ownCloud version 8 is the latest version available for installation.

You may already have a few things that you require installed if have you followed the previous chapters. In case you need a few extra packages, it is best to go through the entire installation process from the beginning as described here.

Requirements

ownCloud requires a database storage engine, PHP, a web server, and data. As usual, I recommend to use nginx as it is lightweight and powerful. You can learn how to install nginx in *Chapter 4*, *Using Fast Web Servers and Databases*. It is also recommended by the developers of ownCloud to use nginx as the web server.

To be able to access ownCloud from the **World Wide Web** (**WWW**), refer to the dynamic DNS section in *Chapter 2*, *Preparing a Network*.

MySQL

Update your repositories and install MySQL:

```
sudo apt-get update
sudo apt-get install mysql-server
```

During installation, you will be asked to set a root `mysql` password on a blue screen.

 Use a strong password and save it into a program such as `Keepass` so that you can quickly recover it for the next time you need it.

After installation, we will enter into the MySQL database console and create a table for ownCloud. You should replace the `password` in the script with your own strong password:

```
mysql -u root -p


CREATE DATABASE owncloud;
CREATE USER owncloud@localhost IDENTIFIED BY 'password';
GRANT ALL PRIVILEGES ON owncloud.* TO owncloud@localhost;
FLUSH PRIVILEGES;


exit
```

Remember the username, password, and table name if you have changed it, as it will be required in the *First Configuration* section.

nginx and PHP

We will install a variety of packages for PHP followed by nginx as follows:

1. Run the following command:

   ```
   sudo apt-get install php5-mysql openssl ssl-cert php5-cli php5-
   common php5-cgi php-pear php-apc curl libapr1 libtool php5-curl
   libcurl4-openssl-dev php-xml-parser php5-dev php5-gd memcached
   php5-memcache


   sudo apt-get install php5-fpm nginx
   ```

2. After you have installed all the required packages, you can create a new `web` folder, download the latest version of ownCloud, and unpack it to a new folder called owncloud:

```
sudo mkdir -p /var/www/owncloud

cd /var/www

sudo wget https://download.owncloud.org/community/owncloud-
8.1.3.tar.bz2

sudo tar -xvf owncloud-8.1.3.tar.bz2

sudo chown -R www-data:www-data /var/www
```

3. We will generate a self-signed certificate, but you can get a free certificate from `https://letsencrypt.org`. A self-signed certificate will show up an error message on your browser, but all your traffic will still be encrypted after you continue:

```
sudo mkdir -p /etc/nginx/ssl

sudo openssl req -x509 -nodes -days 36500 -newkey rsa:2048 -keyout
/etc/nginx/ssl/owncloud.key -out /etc/nginx/ssl/owncloud.crt
```

4. You will be asked to input various other information during the certificate generation process. You can leave `Country Name`, `State`, `Locality Name`, `Organization`, and so on, blank, but for `Common Name`, you must enter your dynamic DNS address.

5. We will now create and edit the nginx configuration file at `/etc/nginx/sites-available/owncloud`.

6. If you have decided to use a domain name for the WWW access, you will need to adjust the `server_name` property accordingly. The DNS name and the private IP of your Raspberry Pi is as follows:

```
server_name {domain.name.com},{pi's IP};
```

7. For simplicity, I only use my Pi's IP address and not DNS's IP address.

The first server block forces all non-SSL requests to be permanently redirected to the SSL configured server block.

The SSL server block has quite a large configuration area. You can find the text version in the code pack.

If you have other sites running, you should pay attention to the root directive. If you use /var/www/ as the root, you can then simply access the site by adding /owncloud to your URL. If you would like to use your Raspberry Pi solely for ownCloud, you can change the root to /var/www/owncloud/, and then you can access ownCloud with your IP or DNS without adding a subfolder to your URL. I have left as recommended for multi-tenant configuration where you are required to add / owncloud to your URL. You may also choose to set up a subdomain locked to the / owncloud directory, which is a good alternative solution. You should decide on this once as changing it later may break ownCloud:

```
server {
  listen 80;
  server_name 192.168.1.21;
  return 301 https://$server_name$request_uri;  # enforce https
}

server {
  listen 443 ssl;
  server_name 192.168.1.21;
  access_log /var/log/nginx/sitename.access.log;
  error_log /var/log/nginx/sitename.error.log;

  ssl_certificate /etc/nginx/ssl/owncloud.crt;
  ssl_certificate_key /etc/nginx/ssl/owncloud.key;

  # Path to the root of your installation
  root /var/www/;
  client_max_body_size 10G; # set max upload size
  fastcgi_buffers 64 4K;

# Some rewrite rules, more to come later
  rewrite ^/owncloud/caldav((/|$).*)$ /owncloud/remote.php/caldav$1
last;
  rewrite ^/owncloud/carddav((/|$).*)$ /owncloud/remote.php/carddav$1
last;
  rewrite ^/owncloud/webdav((/|$).*)$ /owncloud/remote.php/webdav$1
last;

  # Protecting sensitive files from the evil outside world
  location ~ ^/owncloud/(data|config|\.ht|db_structure.xml|README) {
        deny all;
  }
  # Configure the root location with proper rewrite rules
  location /owncloud/ {
```

```
            rewrite ^/owncloud/.well-known/host-meta /public.
php?service=host-meta last;
            rewrite ^/owncloud/.well-known/host-meta.json /public.
php?service=host-meta-json last;
            rewrite ^/owncloud/.well-known/carddav /remote.php/carddav/
redirect;
            rewrite ^/owncloud/.well-known/caldav /remote.php/caldav/
redirect;
            rewrite ^/owncloud/apps/calendar/caldav.php /remote.php/
caldav/ last;
            rewrite ^/owncloud/apps/contacts/carddav.php /remote.php/
carddav/ last;
            rewrite ^/owncloud/apps/([^/]*)/(.*\.(css|php))$ /index.
php?app=$1&getfile=$2 last;
            rewrite ^(/owncloud/core/doc[^\/]+/)$ $1/index.html;
            try_files $uri $uri/ index.php;
  }
location ~ \.php(?:$|/) {
  fastcgi_split_path_info ^(.+\.php)(/.+)$;
  include fastcgi_params;
  fastcgi_param SCRIPT_FILENAME $document_root$fastcgi_script_name;
  fastcgi_param PATH_INFO $fastcgi_path_info;
  fastcgi_param HTTPS on;
  fastcgi_pass unix:/var/run/php5-fpm.sock;
}
# Optional: set long EXPIRES header on static assets
location ~* \.(?:jpg|jpeg|gif|bmp|ico|png|css|js|swf)$ {
expires 30d;
# Optional: Don't log access to assets
access_log off;
}
}
```

Now you have enable ownCloud and disabled the default configuration if you just installed nginx:

```
sudo ln -s /etc/nginx/sites-available/owncloud /etc/nginx/sites-enabled/
owncloud
sudo unlink /etc/nginx/sites-enabled/default
```

Finally, we need to restart everything for the new configuration to take effect:

```
sudo service nginx restart
sudo service php5-fpm restart
```

Permissions

ownCloud will store all your files as normal files in a directory. It uses the database to index files to improve querying speeds. If, for whatever reason, your ownCloud stops functioning properly, you can still access all the files directly without any complicated recovery procedures.

ownCloud runs under www-data. To fix file permission issues, the easiest solution is to add www-data to the pi group, and then create a subfolder with the www-data owner applied to it:

```
sudo usermod -a -G pi www-data
```

The following two commands require you to add your directory destination depending on how and where you have mounted your file system. We will create a new subdirectory and assign the ownership to www-data. We also need to create a temporary directory for uploaded files:

```
sudo mkdir -p /mnt/{your mount point}/owncloud
sudo chown -R www-data:www-data /mnt/{your mount point}/owncloud

sudo mkdir -p /mnt/{your mount point}/owncloud/tmp
sudo chown -R www-data:www-data /mnt/{your mount point}/owncloud/tmp
```

The first configuration

By this point, everything has been preconfigured for the ownCloud application. The final step, which is only required once, is to run through a step-by-step configuration wizard using your browser:

1. Open your browser and type in the IP address or DNS name of your Raspberry Pi.

2. You will see a certificate error. Depending on the browser you use, you may add this certificate to trusted, or click on the button to continue:

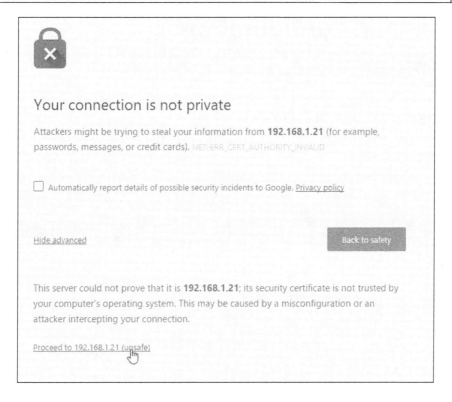

3. If everything went as planned, you will see the initial configuration screen of ownCloud.

4. Type in an Admin username and password (use a strong password as we should not be using this account often). This is the user that will be able to create new users, change configuration, and so on. After creating an admin, we will create a normal user that you should use from here on.

5. The next input asks you about your data folder. This is where you input the directory that we created earlier and set the permission on.

6. In the last step, we need to input the database settings with the username, password, and database that we created earlier. The user name is owncloud (not owncloud@localhost), followed by the password you entered, and the table name of owncloud. Leave the localhost as it is.

7. Finally, we can click on **Finish Setup**. Then, ownCloud will configure the database and test for any issues that may need to be resolved.

After several seconds, you will see the main dashboard presented with a welcome to the ownCloud page, offering several apps to be downloaded and ways to connect to ownCloud.

The admin configuration

If you have just logged in as the admin to the dashboard, it is highly recommended to create a user that you will be using for your daily cloud tasks:

1. In the top-right corner, you will see your admin username and a drop-down menu. Click on it, and then click on **Users**.

2. Before creating a user on this page, click on groups and click on **+ Add Group** to create a new user group, for example, **users**.

3. Now, you can simply type in your username and password; make sure the new group is ticked, and click on **Create**:

By creating a new group, you can now better manage restrictions or options that you would like to use for anybody under this or other new groups later on.

For example, on this page, you can set quotas for each group.

The server admin

While still logged in as admin, click on the admin user name in the top-right corner, and then click on **Admin**. You will land on the sharing options page by default.

On this page, you may notice a few security and set up warnings. If you see anything critical, you can endeavor to resolve the issues by reading the documentation online.

As a standard, there is nothing critical that needs to be changed here, but reading through the available options, you may spot something you like or dislike and adjust it accordingly.

The first option that allows you to tune for groups is **Restrict users to only share with users in their groups**.

When an update is released, you will revisit this page to enable the update mode, and create configuration backups.

You can jump to various sections of the page using the menu on the left.

Installing apps

While logged in as admin via the WebGUI, you can click on the top-left link, which is next to the ownCloud icon. A drop-down menu will appear, and you will see a button to add apps:

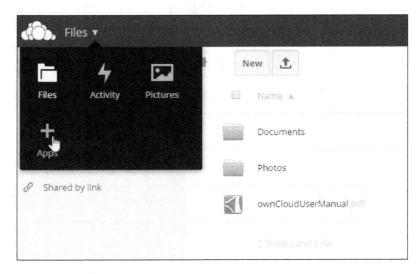

The free edition comes with basic file support and some nice extras. The Enterprise edition comes with official support for **Calendar**, contact management, and synchronization.

On this page, you will see a list-enabled official apps, such as the picture or PDF viewers. There a few more apps that are disabled; to view them click on the **Not Enabled** menu item on the right-hand side.

No need to worry about the lack of apps though, as ownCloud was designed to be extensible. There is a massive collection of user made apps that you can install for free from `https://apps.owncloud.com`.

On the apps page, click on the cog icon in the bottom-left corner, and enable **Experimental Apps** to allow third-party apps to be installed.

If you experience any problems with viewing or starting downloaded apps, you may need to set the **www-data** owner on the folders that you will be creating.

Calendar

To enable calendar functionality on ownCloud, we will install a highly rated app called Calendar Plus:

1. On the `https://apps.owncloud.com` site, search for this app and download it.

2. Extract the zip file into a directory called calendar plus.

3. To install the app, we need to upload the unzipped directory into the `/apps` directory located at `/var/www/owncloud/apps`. Use Filezilla to connect to your Raspberry Pi over SFTP, and upload the directory into the apps directory.

4. In the WebGUI on the **Apps** page, click on **Not Enabled** and find **Calendar+** at the bottom of the page. Click on **Enable**:

Other apps

The `https://apps.owncloud.com` website has an incredible collection of various apps available, and you can install all of them in the same way unless the author provides extra steps in the description of the app.

Daily functionality

If you have checked out the configuration pages, you can log out as admin and log in as the user you have created for yourself using the Web GUI.

For computers and devices running on your local network, you can install the client applications to your desktop or mobile computer and use your internal IP or Pi's DNS.

The World Wide Access

If you have decided to use ownCloud on **WWW** using a dynamic DNS service, the first thing is to check whether it is configured properly. An easy way to do this is to download the client application onto your smart phone or 3G-enabled tablet.

Install the application, and then switch off Wi-Fi to get on to a mobile network, such as 3G. Not all routers support the loopback DNS lookup, which means that trying to access your IP from your IP may fail, but using an external network will verify that your ports have been forwarded properly.

Start the application and enter your details on the login screen. The client application will do a quick connectivity test and inform you about the state.

If you have logged in, you can try and turn your Wi-Fi back on and see if the client will carry on as normal.

Summary

The Raspberry Pi 2 can now be your solution to going independent on cloud storage. As long as you have some redundancy setup on your storage media, you will be able to mostly disconnect from the big corporate giants and gain full control over your data again.

In the next chapter, we will look at using some of the server-side applications, such as databases and nginx, to work with storing GPIO data to monitor the weather.

12
The Internet of Things – Sensors in the Cloud

Now that you have learned the essentials of running software applications on your Raspberry Pi 2, it is time to apply your newly acquired knowledge. This chapter will be about Operating System and agnostic language programming.

Your mission, if you wish to accept it, is to find your favorite flavor of Operating System and programming language while I help you build a foundation on the electrical prototyping.

In this chapter, we will focus on the following topics:

- Understanding power requirements and selecting correct cables
- Working with transistors
- Getting to know **Integrated Circuits** (**IC**) and their purpose
- Windows IoT, events, and real-time systems
- Working with the Cloud for the IoT integration

These topics will expand your basic electronics knowledge and show your good prototyping practices that can be used on any embedded platform, such as your Raspberry Pi 2.

Ultimate decisions on the software completely depend on your own personal preferences. By doing this, you will gain confidence in problem solving and appreciate the vast amount of tools and resources available on the Internet.

If you ever get stuck on a software problem, the best solution is to take a 90-minute break away from your computer, or go to bed and come back to it the next day. If it seems like you are stuck on a particular software problem for days, consider asking your question differently. Do not get hung up on one particular way, as your problem has, most probably, already been solved, and there is already a great solution to it out there.

What is IoT?

The Internet of Things are *things* with sensors that are embedded with electronics and software. The things are connected to a network, most likely the Internet.

The Internet of Things started with machine-to-machine devices, such as alarm systems or GPS trackers, and slowly expanded to home convenience gadgets, such as power grid monitoring tools or some form of home automation.

> *"Experts estimate that the IoT will consist of almost 50 billion objects by 2020."*

> *– Wikipedia*

To build a successful IoT device, you will need to learn about software, the essentials of which are covered in this book. You also need to learn about electronics, which will also be covered in this chapter.

Ohm's law

Ohm's law is a fundamental concept to try and understand before you venture into the prototyping world. One of the main reasons Ohm's law is so widely misunderstood is because it has various equations that originate from a single, mathematical equation.

You can find more information about this diagram and Ohm's law in *Chapter 9, Running Your Pi from a Battery's Power Source*. I have included this diagram here for quick reference as I will demonstrate how to use some of the provided equations:

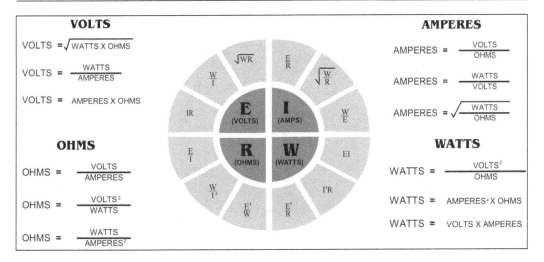

How much power?

In Ohm's law, power (**W**) is know as **watts**. Understanding how to calculate watts is pretty much the most important question that you should be able to answer easily.

For example, what size cable do I need?

- Cables are rated at how many amps they can carry. If you know how many amps you require, then you know which cable to use.

> If you select an incorrect cable size, this usually results in electrical fires, as friction will heat these cables up until they melt and eventually ignite.

To work out how many watts (W) a device uses, you will typically multiply volts (E) by amps (I).

> Watts = Volts x Amps (**W = EI**)

- 5 volts x 1 amp = 5 watts (such as the Raspberry Pi)
- If you have a device that requires 60 watts and is rated for 240 volts, then you can work out these amps by dividing watts by volts.

[Amps = Watts / Volts (**I = W/E**)]

- 60 watts / 240 volts = 0.25 amps (this is a light bulb)
- Once you know how many amps you need to transfer, you can use an **American Wire Gauge (AWG)** table to check the size of cable that you will require over the distance needed:

		American Wire Guage (AWG)									
Length (feet)	Length (meters)	Current (amps)									
		5	10	15	20	25	30	40	50	60	70
3	1	18	18	18	18	16	16	16	12	12	12
15	4	16	12	10	10	8	8	6	6	4	4
20	6	14	12	10	8	8	6	6	4	4	4
25	7	14	10	8	8	6	6	4	4	2	2
30	9	12	10	8	6	6	4	4	2	2	2
40	12	12	8	6	6	4	4	2	2	1	1/0
50	15	10	8	6	4	4	2	2	1	1/0	1/0
60	18	10	6	6	4	2	2	1	1/0	2/0	2/0
70	21	10	6	4	2	2	2	1/0	2/0	2/0	3/0
80	24	8	6	4	2	2	1	1/0	2/0	3/0	3/0
90	27	8	4	4	2	1	1/0	2/0	3/0	3/0	4/0

[It is always recommended to go a size lower (thicker cable) if you are close to the limit of the cable. This is generally within 10% of the capacity.]

Here is an illustration of the how the AWG size works and a conversion to metric millimeters for radius and millimeters squared for the area:

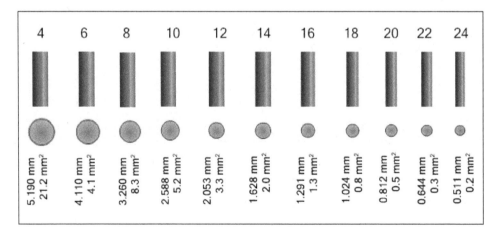

Higher voltage is your friend over longer distances. Generally, the higher the voltage, the thinner the cable you need to use to supply the same amount of amps, reducing the cost of the cable.

 In most cases, the highest voltage that we can use is what is supplied to our home grid 110v/220v, and this will still be the most efficient way to transport power for distances up to 300 feet (100 meters).

You will find this useful in many projects that you are ready to put into *production* away from your prototyping bench. For example, to power remote devices, such as a weather station that controls an irrigation system 120 meters away from the nearest socket, but it may as well be something in your loft, connected within one box:

- Raspberry Pi 2: 5 volts 1 amp
- USB GPRS Modem: 5 volts 0.8 amp
- Medium water pump: 24 volts 2.5 amp
- 6 x Solenoids: 9 volts 1 amp
- Relay board: 12 volts 0.5 amp

You will learn how to apply Ohm's law and use IC to deal with this problem efficiently later in this chapter.

Choosing sensors

The answer to this question depends on what you want to build. Sensors come as a variety of packages, operated by various voltages, and interfaced with some kind of communication standard.

Resistors, fuses, and diodes

These are typically the easiest elements of electrical design to understand. If you are planning to create a device, you should find a basic electronics course to gain good understanding of these basics before continuing.

Transistors

Everybody that uses a computer will have probably heard of a transistor. What is a transistor really? It is a semiconductor device that can be used to amplify or switch electronic signals and electrical power. A semiconductor is a solid substance that can conduct electricity when a certain condition has been met; otherwise they act as an insulator.

Their packages are easily identified as they usually consist of three wires (legs). These legs are named Base (b), Collector (c), and Emitter (e):

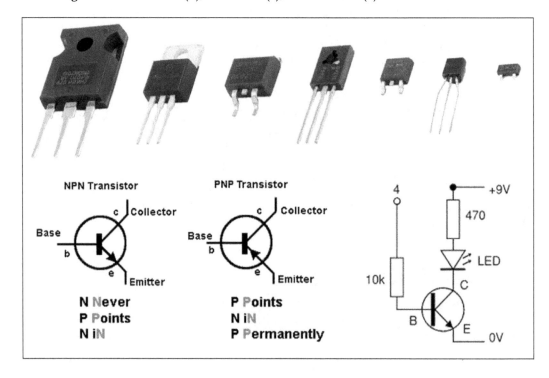

The preceding illustration shows various packages that a transistor can be found in. The ones that look like they have two legs, actually have their base on the other side.

The illustration also shows two different types of transistors: **NPN** and **PNP**. They essentially do the same thing, but NPN transistors are used to switch higher voltages and PNP lower voltage than what's used in your main circuit. Also, PNP transistors are *turned on* when pulling the base low while NPN is *turned on* when you provide a voltage to the base.

Usually, in prototyping, we are mostly interested in switching higher voltages, and from here on, we will be working with NPN transistors.

It may sound confusing at first, but just think of a transistor as a plain old switch. When you apply the correct amount of current to an NPN transistor's base, it is like your finger pushing a button. Once you get to the correct pressure, the switch will turn on, and the current will flow through the collector to the emitter. The amount of power (A) used to trigger a transistor is typically very low and sage for the GPIO's on the Raspberry Pi.

Looking at the sample circuit (bottom right) in the illustration, you can see a 9v power source connected to a resistor, LED, and then to the collector of the transistor. The emitter is connected to GND. This is pretty much how you will wire a switch. In the digital world, to turn on this switch, we need an extra input—**base**. For example, we will use GPIO PIN 4. This can be an output from any kind of embedded device with a 3.3v, 5.0v, or a higher voltage. The maximum voltage depends on the resistor's technical specification.

The 10k resistor can be of any value between 1K and 20K, and it should always be connected before the base of the transistor. The resistor is there to limit the maximum current that flows through the base of the transistor, preventing damage to the transistor.

Once the I/O is set high in software, the *switch* will close and the LED will illuminate.

 You just learned the basics of transistors. As you build more designs, you will find new circuits that require a combination of transistors to achieve a specific goal.

Using transistors in such a way makes switching other voltages much easier from an embedded platform, using a low amount of current.

You should always try and find the transistor marking, and you should search for its datasheet to understand the minimum and maximum values it can handle. The datasheet will also provide the minimum current required on the base to turn it on.

Transistors are typically used in low-voltage designs. To turn on high voltage, such as 220 volts, you should almost always use a relay. Yes, you can use the transistor to turn the relay on.

Integrated Circuit Packages

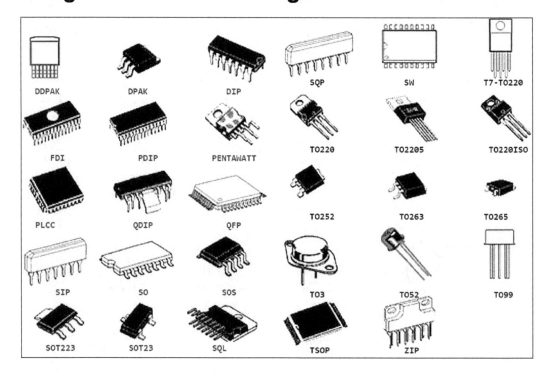

These are a variety of other IC packages that you will find. You should be able to use any of these with nothing more than a soldering iron or breadboard.

[Other packages such as QFN require specialist equipment to be prototyped with. An example of such a package is BCM2836, and it can be found on your Raspberry Pi 2.]

Putting it all together

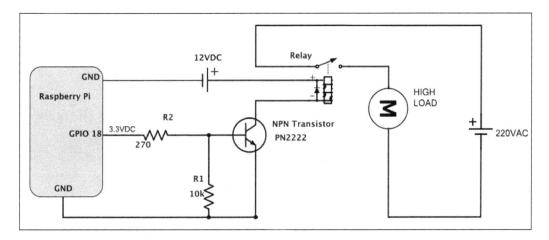

This circuit demonstrates switching a high-voltage 48 volt DC motor.

 Be very careful when working with high voltages. Incorrect wiring will cause irreparable damage. Switching mains voltages may be lethal, and please do not attempt this if you are in doubt.

Accurate data using Arduino

The Raspberry Pi typically runs on event-driven Operating Systems. This mean that a queue of events gets processed by the processor as fast as the processor can handle it. Unfortunately, even if your processor is idle, there is still an overhead in the event system that causes significant problems with real-time sensors or applications.

There are real-time Operating Systems for the Raspberry Pi, but this will severely limit the capabilities that you have learned to use and love. Real-time Operating systems guarantee that an action, such as some code, will be completed in the predefined time. A very popular Operating System for these types of simple yet extremely accurate tasks is the Arduino family IC. They are amongst the best for doing millions of tasks over and in a very precise time.

We will look at some examples of how an Arduino IC will help you gather data by showing a use case of building a weather station.

Building a weather station

A great project to work on is building a weather station. The Raspberry Pi 2 has so much processing power to offer:

- It can store a large amount of data in a database with ease
- It can be its own web server running with a variety of programming languages
- It can crunch numbers, create statistics, and eventually become nice graphs
- It can even stream live videos using WebRTC or RTSP

Real-time embedded devices

Atmel AVR (used on Arduino) and PICAXE are very well-known microcontrollers that run code with real-time precision. The advantage of these microcontrollers is that you can program them with simple code once, upload the code, disconnect them from the development board, and use them like a standalone IC.

Your initial cost for a development board maybe about the same as a Raspberry Pi on its own, but after this, getting the programmable **Microcontroller Unit** (**MCU**) will cost a few dollars, and will be even cheaper for tiny versions.

There are expansion boards available for some of these embedded devices, mostly for Arduino.

The data communication

Real-time devices also offer very precise or faster data communication between various other devices by not only offering hardware interfaces but also software bit banging.

 Bit banging is a technique for any kind of serial communication using software instead of some dedicated hardware.

Real-time events

The essential benefit of an MCUs is that you would require it when building a weather station is required when counting time sensitive actions, such as wind speed, which must be calculated every second without any delay.

You write a small function of code that executes when a selected pin is triggered. This is known as an interrupt. This code is as simple as incrementing a counter.

The main program is an endless loop of code or an internal-timed interrupt. Not all MCUs offer internal-timed interrupts, but what is critical is that it always runs at a selected time, for example, every 60 seconds. On an MCU, this is guaranteed to run every 60 seconds to the microsecond. This is crucial to make sure that you can run an algorithmic function, which uses your wind counter to save the wind speed. On an event driven OS, you may get highly inaccurate readings caused by delayed processor queues or the optimized execution.

Analog inputs

The Raspberry Pi lacks analog inputs. MCUs usually have more analog inputs than digital ones. On tiny versions, they may even completely lack digital inputs.

Analog inputs will be very useful to read the direction of the wind, as wind vanes usually output a calculated subvoltage from the input voltage to inform you of the direction. Something like a potentiometer, but more simply, it is like various resistors connected to a reed switch, which will activate a given circuit.

There are still a lot of other applications that can be useful for analog inputs.

Parts required

The most affordable and pretty complete package is offered by Sparkfun—a wind vane, anemometer, and rain counter, with cables and a complete installation mount. Adding extras to this, such as instruments to measure UV light, atmospheric pressure, and temperature, is a breeze.

You will also need a Raspberry Pi and a programmed Arduino MCU or similar.

Storing data on the Cloud

At some point of any project, you will, most certainly, want to store collected data somewhere. Usually, this is from collecting sensors, but it could also be debugging data.

The Cloud is a network of servers that can provision virtual machines for any use. Usually, you start from one server, but you always have the ability to increase the size or bundle several virtual machines to act as one endpoint. All this is usually handled by a nice frontend, such as Azure, Amazon AWS, or the Google Cloud platform.

Phant

Phant is a logging tool developed by Sparkfun Electronics and is ready to be used free of charge at `https://data.sparkfun.com`; it stores data in JSON format. JSON is easy to read and compress, but most importantly, it's dynamic; dynamic meaning that you don't build relationships between each data packet, as in traditional SQL servers. This means that each data packet can contain any variety of structures that you save to Phant.

You can find yourself a very cheap Linux-based virtual machine and install your own Phant platform to take full control of your cloud data. This is an extremely easy way to allow you access to shared data anywhere in the world, as long as you have an Internet connection.

Summary

In this chapter, you learned the basics of electrical engineering and the external system's integration. The possibilities are endless and only confined to your own imagination. In case you ever seem to get stuck, it is worth visiting some of these great sites for more information.

For Stack Exchange, use the following:

- Electrical Engineering: `http://electronics.stackexchange.com/`
- Raspberry Pi: `http://raspberrypi.stackexchange.com/`
- Stack Overflow (Programming): `http://stackoverflow.com/`
- Ask Ubuntu (Linux related): `http://askubuntu.com/`

For other sites, use the following:

- Arduino Forums: `https://forum.arduino.cc/`
- PICAXE Forums: `http://www.picaxeforum.co.uk/`
- Searching the internet

Thank you for your interest in this book, and I wish you happy prototyping!

Index

V

VC-1 36
virtual directory
  URL 44
VisualGDB
  about 91
  URL 91
Visual Studio
  about 112
  application, deploying 116
  debugging 116
  debugging, breakpoints 117
  debugging, unhandled exceptions 118
  Hello World application 113-115
  samples 119
  Visual Studio 2015, installing 112, 113
voltage regulator
  about 104
  discharge characteristics 107
  discharge curves 106
  Ohms law 104-106

W

weather station
  about 8
  analog inputs 143
  building 142
  data communication 142
  parts 143
  real-time embedded devices 142
  real-time events 142, 143
web conferencing 85, 86
WebRTC
  about 83
  streaming 83, 84

Windows 10 IoT WebGUI
  about 119
  startup app, setting 119
WinSCP
  connecting with 64
  URL 64, 65
Wireless configuration (Wi-Fi)
  about 17
  console, setting up from 18-21
  desktop, setting up from 18
  wicd-curses, using 21, 22
  wireless adapters 17, 18
Wireless USB network adapters 5
wlan0 interface 17
World Wide Access (WWW) 131
World Wide Web (WWW) 121

X

xboxdrv 7
X desktop
  streaming 86

www.ingramcontent.com/pod-product-compliance
Lightning Source LLC
LaVergne TN
LVHW081343050326
832903LV00024B/1292